SAVE AMERICA

LIVES ARE AT STAKE

ACTS ONE EIGHT
Publishing

SAVE AMERICA

LIVES ARE AT STAKE

STEVEN ANDREW

Paperback ISBN-13: 9780977955084

eBook: ISBN-13: 9780977955046

Copyright © 2016 by Steven Andrew   Update November 2017

Published by ACTS ONE EIGHT Publishing™
ActsOneEightPublishing.com

Contents

Christian Resources

༄∽ఴ

I Am Praying for You

God wants to protect you, those close to you, and our beloved country. Soon you will discover the safety, hope, and blessings that come by saving the USA. You will know God better, and He will be glorified in your life and in our Christian nation. With love, care, and joy, I am praying for you to walk close with God.

God has blessed me with exceptional people to review the manuscripts. I thank God for each skilled person. May God strengthen each of you in Him!

༄∽ఴ

Note on Book Versions

"Save America" is an expanded version of my book "Jesus Makes America Great," and it focuses on God's protection, with more detailed teaching.

Preface

The 9-11 Cross testifies of God's covenant through Jesus Christ with the USA. The 17 foot steel beam cross was found whole and then displayed.

"...hope in His mercy." Psalm 147:11 KJV

We live in dangerous times with nuclear war threats, the possibility of an economic collapse, and terrorism, but America has a breakthrough secret to bring God's supernatural power to protect our lives and the USA. In fact, every blessing in our nation's history has come from following *7 Specific Bible Truths,* which we will learn in this book.

These promises from God's Word are the most effective actions for you to follow to have security and they are the reason the USA attained Christian freedom in 1776. Scripture shows these *7 Bible Truths* give you the only answer to go from dangers to safety.

You are now going to discover how God's covenant mercy protects you and spares the USA from a final judgment, where millions of people would perish.

Will you join me to Save America? I hope you will.

Steven Andrew
Pastor, USA Christian Church
www.USA.church

1

Millions of Lives Are at Stake

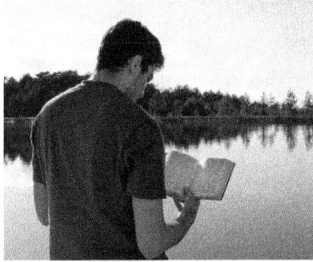

"Go, inquire of the LORD..."
2 Chronicles 34:21 KJV

This book of hope gives you answers from the Word of God to protect yourself and your loved ones. It exposes real dangers that you must know, and then it gives you the most powerful Scriptural solution that always turns things around.

We are in a great emergency situation. A Biblical analysis of the news shows that lives are at stake. The USA's future is in question. We have seen the judgment of God for our nation's sins and there have been unprecedented national dangers.

We must stop this while we can—before it is too late and there is a final judgment, as Israel experienced. Only the Word of God gives us the true answers to secure our safety, freedom, and financial stability. Saving the USA is of utmost importance, because there are valuable things to gain or lose. Our personal and national destinies are at stake, including:

- Christian liberty or persecution
- Peace or wars
- Happiness or suffering
- Financial prosperity or economic collapse
- Life or death
- Strong families or broken homes
- Americanism or globalism

Consider Israel and the USA

The people of Israel got to the point where they wouldn't listen to God and keep covenant with Him. They just lived like the world did. Yet, danger was all around them. Israel didn't realize God's Word said their lives were in jeopardy. Any day they could see God's final judgment.

In mercy, God reached out His hand to forgive Israel. But the people didn't think they needed mercy. They believed God was tolerant of sinful ways and that He could be ignored.

Then it happened: Israel was invaded by Assyria. The people went from living normal lives to losing everything.

Years later, the southern kingdom of Judah would drift from God. However, Kings Asa and Josiah, and the people, reaffirmed covenant to follow the LORD, which is what this book is about. As a result, they found God's mercy. They went from troubles and the danger of captivity to living in peace and having blessed lives (2 Chronicles 15 & 34).

For the USA, we are also in a dangerous place. So, we must avoid God's final judgment. While we look at God's discipline, hold onto hope, as we will learn how to bring our lives from perils to safety by following *7 Specific Bible Truths.*

God Is Holy and Our Judge

We are to live with a holy reverence of the LORD, because He is the Judge of all the earth. God judges righteously and opposes evil. Like parents reward or discipline a child if they follow their instructions, God blesses or disciplines based on obedience of His Word. The Bible says, *Be not deceived; God is not mocked* and explains that sowing sin results in reaping corruption (Galatians 6:7-8 KJV).

Abraham Lincoln said, *by His divine law, nations like individuals are subjected to punishments and chastisements...*[1] An American belief is that God is the Judge of nations, because God says, *When the land sins against Me... then will I stretch out Mine hand upon it* (Ezekiel 14:13 KJV).

Judgments take many forms, such as the rise in power of anti-Christian forces, freedoms being attacked, financial loss, and the sword. But God has great compassion for us! That is why He gives certain events *for a sign and for a wonder* that we would know when He judges us (Deuteronomy 28:46 KJV).

Good leaders that care for our well-being and protect liberty are God's blessing, but bad politicians (the swamp) are a sign of God's judgment (Judges 2:11 - 4:2). God tries to get our attention with politicians who don't listen to the people, act as dictators, misuse our resources for globalization, and oppose our founders. In the USA, we have the freedom to choose Christian representatives. Yet, many people have voted for anti-American politicians who oppose our God-given rights and put the country's security at risk. Unless voters follow God's Word in choosing leaders, they can be deceived by a lying spirit to their harm (2 Chronicles 18:18-22).

One of the USA's national security assets is the control of the Internet, which we created. This gives us uncensored web access, but Barack Obama jeopardized our country by surrendering the control of the Internet to the UN. Foreign governments controlling the Internet undermines our access and freedom. The Republican Congress did not stop Obama.[2]

Think of the times that Obama and others have persecuted Christians, opposed the right to bear arms, and spied on innocent Americans. These acts illustrate hatred of the First, Second, and Fourth Amendments. Obama and Hillary Clinton refused to say the USA's National Motto is *In God We Trust,* but lied it is *e pluribus unim.*[3] Consider the alarming Wikileaks news that the same Muslim countries funding ISIS funded Clinton.[4]

The reason for these and other acts against the USA is corrupt leaders are God's discipline for: (1) National disobedience to the Word of God and (2) Covenant breaking acts, such as taking daily Bible reading out of schools and millions of abortions. *...if ye shall despise my statutes, or if your soul abhor my judgments, so that ye will not do all my commandments, but that ye break my covenant: I also will do this unto you...* **they that hate you shall reign over you;** (Leviticus 26:14-17 KJV). This is why people said Obama and Hillary hate America. They colluded with Russia as traitors and gave away 20% of our uranium. Millions of people in the USA could die from a nuclear bomb because of this.

President Donald Trump

President Trump says he loves America, so we see God ended part of this judgment. Yet, when Congress, courts and

10

the media oppose the President following God, we know the judgment is not fully over.

God is using President Trump. As Christians, we thank God the president says, "In America we worship God, not government," is pro-life, quotes the Bible, calls for pastors to speak freely and wants Congress to "destroy" the Johnson Amendment that has silenced non-profit churches. Christians support President Trump where he follows Jesus Christ!

Because of the people living out the powerful *7 Bible Truths,* God withheld His anger for our national sins and stopped Clinton. Those who obeyed God's Word brought God's mercy that would have been lost with Hillary.

Some people think that politicians are in control, but God is the one who blesses or judges the nation. By the sovereignty of God, He directs leaders based on the nation's obedience to Him. *The king's heart is in the hand of the LORD, as the rivers of water: he turns it whithersoever he will* (Proverbs 21:1 KJV).

Others think we can be idle and sit back with President Trump, but the church not working to advance the Kingdom of our Lord Jesus Christ would mean more corruption. It is a strong church that causes the USA to be great. The biggest mistake people can make with President Trump is to trust in man instead of God, which means ruin.

Invasion, Captivity, and Destruction

The real issue to pay attention to is whether we are pleasing God and have His blessings or if we are provoking

God to wrath and see judgment on our nation. He gives different judgments for different sins. False gods and sodomite societies result in the strongest judgments of losing wars, captivity, and removal. History records these judgments happened to Israel. For this reason, it is urgent to understand that the nation's greatest danger is sin.

Those who forget God and *walk after other gods... shall surely perish* (Deuteronomy 8:19 KJV). The tolerance of false gods is a common sin and rightfully angers God. Muslims deny that God has a Son. The Bible says that such a denial is "antichrist" (1 John 2:22 KJV). Yet, Obama, Clinton, and the Democrat Party prayed often with Muslims, joining with them in worshipping a god who opposes Jesus Christ. Christianity and Islam are very different. Jesus Christ teaches to "love your enemies" and be "wise" to avoid them harming you. However, the Koran teaches to kill Christians, Jews, and others. That is why Muslims have a history of violence.

It is not just Democrats, but Republicans have prayed with other gods. There were Muslim and Sikh prayers at the 2016 GOP National Convention[5] and the National Cathedral had Hindu, Mormon, Islamic, and other non-Christian speakers after Trump's inauguration.[5] The Bible says interfaith prayer causes God's wrath, as when people served Baal and Molech.

Some say it is tolerance to accept those with other gods, but God's Word reveals this sin has put our lives and nation in danger of God's judgment of war. There is a common misconception that other religions, such as Mormonism, are good. We see most pastors are silent that the GOP chair is a Mormon cult member (Mitt Romney's niece). Mormons believe the evil lies that God was first a man and Jesus is the spirit brother of Lucifer. How can blaspheming God be good?

God says, Sodom and Gomorrah *giving themselves over to fornication, and going after strange flesh, are set forth for an example, suffering the vengeance of eternal fire* (Jude 7 KJV). God's judgment for same-sex marriage could be brimstone and fire, a nuclear war, or other destruction (Genesis 19:24).

Yet, Obama, the Clintons, the Supreme Court, schools, the military, and others have provoked God with homosexual and transgender sin, which God says is "abomination" (Leviticus 18:22, Deuteronomy 22:5). For example, the Air Force relieved a Senior Master Sergeant of duty for refusing to support the beliefs of a lesbian commander.[4]

Terrorism Is a Judgment for Sin

Safety is God's blessing. Yet, one of the judgments that has not ended is terrorism. The Bible says false gods, same-sex marriage, and other sins are what cause terrorism. Terror is a curse from disregarding God's Word and covenant breaking acts. *If... ye will not do all My commandments, but that ye break My covenant: I also will do this unto you; **I will even appoint over you terror*** (Leviticus 26:14-16 KJV).

Just weeks after the Democrats and Republicans prayed with false gods at the 2016 national conventions, three Muslim terrorist attacks occurred within a 12 hour period. First, the Minnesota Mall stabbings, with 8 people wounded. Then the New York City and New Jersey bombings that injured 29 more people.[6] After this, a Republican Congress refused to stop Obama bringing in thousands more Muslim refugees who don't assimilate, including the Ohio State University terrorist who attacked people.

The Ft. Lauderdale airport shootings were by an Islamic convert and killed five people and wounded six others. This happened after it was announcement the National Cathedral would pray with false gods. Learning why these judgments occur also explains why Obama and the "Department of Homeland Security" (DHS) brought Muslim terrorists to the country, but then the DHS defied logic by calling citizens who are Christians, pro-life, and veterans as potential terrorists.[7]

While we want to end terrorism, no amount of money or military strikes will make it go away until we obey God's Word and repent of covenant breaking acts against God.

Foreigners Rising Higher and Taking Jobs Away

Terrorists, gangs, and those with contagious diseases have crossed our unprotected border. This is God's judgment. *The bloody city... full of lies and robbery... because of the multitude of the whoredoms... witchcrafts...* ***the gates of thy land shall be set wide open unto thine enemies*** (Nahum 3:13 KJV).

In Idaho, three Muslim migrants held a five year old girl at knife point, threatened to kill her, gang raped, and urinated on the beautiful girl.[8] This judgment is also why American flags have been banned and America Day was cancelled at Jackson Hole High School in Wyoming—to not offend students from other countries.[10]

Good jobs for the USA and a nation united in Christ are a blessing. However, *if thou wilt not hearken unto the voice of the LORD thy God... The fruit of thy land, and all thy labours, shall a nation which thou knowest not eat up; and thou shalt be only oppressed and crushed alway... **The stranger that is within thee shall get up above thee very high; and thou shalt come down very low.*** (Deuteronomy 28:15, 33, 43 KJV)

Did God speak through Trump while campaigning to end this judgment and to protect the USA? He said:

Donald J. Trump is calling for a total and complete shutdown of Muslims entering the United States until our country's representatives can figure out what is going on. According to Pew Research, among others, there is great hatred towards Americans by large segments of the Muslim population. Most recently, a poll from the Center for Security Policy released data showing "25% of those polled agreed that violence against Americans here in the United States is justified as a part of the global jihad" and 51% of those polled, "agreed that Muslims in America should have the choice of being governed according to Shariah." Shariah authorizes such atrocities as murder against non-believers who won't convert, beheadings and more unthinkable acts that pose great harm to Americans, especially women. [11]

Of the new jobs added before President Trump, about half went to foreign-born workers since 2009.[12] As more people say, "America first", we see God wants to end this judgment.

"The Worst of the Heathen" as Enemies

The USA's enemies have lined up against us. China, North Korea, ISIS, Iran, sinners, corrupt businesses, and others have made threats. An attack by brutal people is God's judgment. *I will bring the worst of the heathen* (Ezekiel 7:24 KJV) *a nation of fierce countenance, which shall not regard the old, nor show favor to the young* (Deuteronomy 28:49-50 KJV).

Liberty is God's blessing, but tyranny and communism are God's discipline. *[W]e are servants... for the land that thou gavest unto our fathers... we are servants in it: And it yieldeth much increase unto the kings whom thou hast set over us because of our sins: also they have dominion over our bodies, and over our cattle, at their pleasure, and we are in great distress.* (Nehemiah 9:34-37 KJV).

We saw this especially with Obama, who honored the Chinese communist who murdered 50 to 80 million people, by putting a Mao Zedong ornament on the White House Christmas tree.[13] The Empire State Building lit up with red and yellow lights for communist China[14]. Inside the USA, anti-American China trained with our military.[15]

Privacy is under attack by a police state monitoring everything. Automobiles are tracked and our personal phone calls and web browsing are unconstitutionally monitored.[16, 17]

God-given Rights Opposed by Homosexuals

God's people have been attacked by those who hate Jesus Christ. As you may have heard, Christian florists, bakers, clerks, and workers have been unjustly fined, jailed, or fired for following God. In Alabama, Judge Roy Moore, who stands boldly for traditional marriage, was unjustly suspended from being Chief Justice.[18] Kim Davis, a county clerk in Kentucky, was unfairly and wrongly jailed for following her conscience to oppose same-sex marriage.[19]

Disobeying the Constitution Is Lawlessness

Congress, the Supreme Court, Obama, and others have violated the Constitution in many ways. An example is the Supreme Court gave the unjust opinion to remove the ban on same-sex marriage[20] that God and our founders established.

In response, Mike Huckabee explained that same-sex marriage "is not law," because the Supreme Court has no Constitutional authority to make laws. Yet, many are deceived that "judicial tyranny" is legal. We know the Constitution says Congress makes laws and the president signs them.[21]

Businesses and Politicians Bullying Christians

Many corporations hate God, who says transgender sin is "abomination" (Deuteronomy 22:5, Romans 1:30). PayPal and others cut jobs from North Carolina for not allowing men to use women's bathrooms.[22] Even with rape and privacy dangers, Target and politicians, such as the new North Carolina governor, oppose having only women use women's bathrooms. Men have secretly filmed women in dressing rooms at Target[23] and the family is breaking down.

Unbelievers persecuting Christians in the USA is because of God's people turning to them in business and politics. *She was mine; and she doted on her lovers... Wherefore **I have delivered her into the hand of her lovers*** (Ezekiel 23:5, 9 KJV).

Schools Teaching Children to Lose Their Souls

Our children are in jeopardy with schools destroying the lives of the youth with sin. Teachers used to explain to *love the Lord your God... is the first, the great, the indispensable duty of every rational being* and that *sin is the source of all evil,*[24] but schools typically censor God and instruct about evil ways.

Teachers indoctrinate students with abortion, pre-marital sex, sodomy, and the lies of evolution. Our consciences should convict us about this. Teachers and people who do not follow Jesus Christ make sinful citizens and end up in hell. As a result, academics are low. The USA ranks below the world average in math, below Vietnam, and just average in reading, lower than Chinese Taipai.[25] Parents should be concerned.

A Weakened Military

The U.S. military has not been able to win a war in a small country such as Iraq. The military has removed crosses, bullied Christians, and shamefully allowed homosexual sin in the ranks. An unjust court blocked President Trump's transgender military ban and a Marine was convicted at a court martial for keeping a Bible verse in her workspace.[26]

How can God go out with our armies if they mock Him? Provoking God to wrath is the greatest threat to our military and our safety (Psalm 60:10). We are in a desperate state.

The Danger of a Financial Collapse

The financial mess that Obama and others handed to President Trump is worse than many realize.[27] The USA went from having more than half the wealth of the world to having nearly 80% of the people live near poverty, with joblessness or a reliance on welfare. Lower paying jobs, fewer middle class households, high taxes, and the staggering national debt are signs of economic judgment.[28] On the other hand, God's blessing is the economy improving.

A nation disregarding God means the curse of *thou shalt not prosper in thy ways* (Deuteronomy 28:29 KJV). The USA's money has been plundered by spoilers. They *rejected His statutes, and His covenant that He made with their fathers... they... went after the heathen... and worshipped all the host of heaven... they caused their sons and their daughters to pass through the fire, and used divination...* **Therefore the LORD... delivered them into the hand of spoilers** (2 Kings 17:15-20 KJV).

We heard God's mercy to end this judgment in President Trump's inauguration speech. The president said, *"[we] spent trillions of dollars overseas... We've made other countries rich while the wealth, strength, and confidence of our country has disappeared over the horizon. One by one, the factories shuttered and left our shores..."* It is God, who is using Trump, to help Americans and end the spoiling of the nation's wealth.

The final economic outcome is dependent on the USA's obedience to God. If our nation won't follow the Bible, there will be hard times, jobs will be lost, and enemies may invade us. But if we obey God, there will be Biblical prosperity.

One of the other judgments to mention is damage to the earth and animals. Sin is the greatest cause of eco-devastation. Environmental ruin came by Noah's flood, Egypt's plagues, and Sodom and Gomorrah's destruction, due to the people's wickedness, thinking on evil, homosexual sin, and rebellion to God (Genesis 6:5-17; 19:24-28, Exodus 7:14-11:10).

Sin Causes the USA's Problems

God cares for us and He wants to protect us, so He let's us know the real cause for our national troubles is disobeying Him. It is one thing to unintentionally sin and then confess it to God and be forgiven, but to not repent or to publicly oppose Him is serious. Things won't be better until we deal with the sins causing God's judgment and Biblical curses.

While we have restored some of God's favor, the country can't be great without more repentance of the sins causing God's judgment and Biblical curses. Sin affects our safety, strength, and prosperity, so it must be addressed across the nation, in churches, dinner conversations, and everywhere. God's judgment comes from the people opposing Him with:

- False gods
- Homosexuality, adultery, and fornication
- Not calling for Christian religious liberty
- Not standing up for our God-given rights
- Rebellion to God's sovereignty in our government
- Helping the ungodly in politics and business
- Abortion
- Coveting (wanting other people's items, greed)
- The occult, sorcery, and witchcraft

How can our lives truly improve without ending these harmful ways? How can we say we are friends of God if we act against Him as an enemy? To make the USA great again, we must search our hearts, see if there are any sins to turn from, and have national repentance of all wickedness.

We cannot be deceived if the media downplays sin as just social issues or a culture war. Sin is treason against God. For example, the news often says the focus is the economy instead of doing God's will, but God says sin is what causes an economic collapse.

Some think that God's chastisement is an Old Testament idea. They say we live in New Testament times where its about forgiveness and grace. While Jesus' sacrifice does provide forgiveness and God's grace, it does not eliminate God's discipline (Hebrews 12:4-11).

Jesus teaches that judgment comes to those not repenting (Rev. 2:20-23 & 3:19). He told one man to *sin no more, lest a worse thing come unto thee* (John 5:14 KJV). From Genesis to Revelation, God instructs us that sin causes His discipline.

This reveals that the true battle to save the USA is between those following Jesus Christ and those against the Lord. The right opposing the left and the left opposing the right is not God's plan, for both tolerate some of these sins.

We Can Have Safe and Blessed Lives

It doesn't have to be this way where we live with millions of lives at stake and the danger of captivity or removal. The choice is ours. It is encouraging to recall others ended God's discipline. So in this book, we look at three remarkable Bible accounts of God's covenant mercy. They are King Asa, Moses, and King Josiah (2 Chronicles 15, Exodus 32, 2 Chronicles 34).

With so many riots, divisions, wars, and terrorists, there seems to be a similarity for us to King Asa's day when *there was no peace... nation was destroyed of nation, and city of city* (2 Chronicles 15:5-6 KJV). But Asa found hope that God was with Judah while they were with Him; and if they sought Him, He would be found. God would free them of the trouble. Asa knew the LORD was righteous and if they weren't with God, He wouldn't be with them (2 Chronicles 15:2).

When Israel turned to the molten calf they forsook the LORD. God saw this sin as a covenant breaking act. He said to Moses, *let me alone, that my wrath may wax hot against them, and that I may consume them* (Exodus 32:10 KJV).

Since God wanted to show mercy, He allowed Moses to remind Him of covenant with Israel. Then Moses separated the people by finding out who loved God and who didn't by asking: *Who is on the LORD'S side?* (Exodus 32:10-26 KJV). The people who were on the LORD's side were spared.

King Josiah lived in a world where the Word of God was set aside and forgotten. He loved God, so to honor the LORD he commissioned the repairing of God's temple. Suddenly the Law of God was found in the recesses of the temple and the priests brought it to the king. For the first time in his life Josiah heard these words and saw the connection between the nation's sins and God's judgment.

He trembled as he realized that he was not truly honoring God by allowing evil to remain and God was going to bring total destruction for their sin. Seeing that God's judgment was on Judah, he tore his clothes in desperation and fear. He ordered the false gods to be destroyed and led the people to serve the LORD and turn from evil.

When Josiah inquired of God, he discovered their lives were in jeopardy for forsaking God and said, *great is the wrath of the LORD that is poured out upon us, because our fathers have not kept the word of the LORD* (2 Chronicles 34:21 KJV). So King Josiah and the people renewed covenant to live for the LORD and a great revival came.

Will we have the same tender heart of love for God and reaffirm covenant? Amazingly, the revival came after evil King Manasseh forgot God. There is always hope.

God's Favor Comes by Re-affirming Covenant

We can go from danger to safety by agreeing that the USA serves the LORD with our Christian founding fathers, who advise us to follow them by:

- Insisting to have Christian religious liberty.
- Re-affirming covenant that the LORD is the God of our nation and we are His people.

True American leaders always lead us to obey God. John Adams said, *As the safety and prosperity of nations ultimately and essentially depend on the protection and the blessing of Almighty God... the just judgments of God against prevalent iniquity, are a loud call to repentance and reformation...*[29]

Puritan leader John Winthrop, who applied "a city on a hill" to America, said, *If we... shall embrace this present world... then the Lord will surely break out in wrath against us... He will make us know the price of the breach of such a covenant.*[30] To win our liberty, George Washington knew the USA must not provoke God, so he said, *We cannot hope for the blessing of heaven on our army if we insult it by our impiety and folly.*[31]

Following the powerful *7 Bible Truths* that we will now learn is how to eliminate the problems that affect our safety and blessings. God is holy. So a holy covenant with Him saves our lives and give us His favor to live in safety, be protected, save our children's souls, prevent an economic collapse, and defend Christianity to have liberty and peace.

This safeguards our lives and gives us a better quality of life. Be encouraged. God wants to show mercy to the USA. There is more good news. The *7 Bible Truths* are the exact step-by-step plan to make the USA great again. Christians and churches can help *Save America* by teaching these truths. Those who join in covenant are modern day American heroes.

✝ Prayer

Father, You are merciful. We humble
ourselves, get on our knees, and seek Your mercy
to protect our lives, loved ones, and the USA.
In Jesus' name. Amen.

✓ Reflection Questions

1. *What are Biblical examples of God judging nations?*
2. *According to the Word of God, what sins result in invasion, captivity, or destruction?*
3. *Why are you safer when the USA follows God? Explain.*

2

First Truth—Covenant with the True God

The first act of Congress - George Washington, John Adams, Samuel Adams, and our Founding Fathers praying in Jesus' name and reading the Holy Bible in 1774. Washington (center), John Adams (sixth from top left) and Samuel Adams (left of John Adams in light coat).

"Blessed is the nation whose God is the LORD..."

Psalm 33:12 KJV

America is the most amazing story of God orchestrating our country. If your school didn't censor it, you know the Jamestown Settlers' first act was to pray, fast, plant a cross on the Virginia beach, and covenant America to God "to all generations." The first permanent English settlers consecrated America to God forever. **Our covenant from 1607** says:

We do hereby dedicate this Land, and ourselves, to reach the People within these shores with the Gospel of Jesus Christ, and to raise up Godly generations after us, and with these generations take the Kingdom of God to all the earth. May this Covenant of Dedication remain to all generations, as long as this earth remains, and may this Land... be Evangelist to the World. May all who see this Cross, remember what we have done here, and may those who come here to inhabit join us in this Covenant...[1] (Jamestown Settlers, 1607).

The Pilgrims' covenant love for God also gives us hope. The Mayflower Compact reveals our country is God's nation:

IN THE NAME OF GOD, AMEN... Having undertaken for the Glory of God, and Advancement of the Christian Faith... Do by these Presents, solemnly and mutually, in the Presence of God and one another, covenant and combine ourselves together into a civil Body Politick... Anno Domini; 1620.[2]

The Puritans arrived in 1630. Famous John Winthrop wrote, *We are entered into covenant with Him for this work.[3]*

The true American dream is stated with the New England Confederation in 1643. It reminds us that *we all came into these parts of America with one and the same end and aim, namely, to advance the Kingdom of our Lord Jesus Christ and to enjoy the liberties of the Gospel in purity with peace.[4]* Nothing is more American than Christian religious liberty!

Congress Pledged the USA's Allegiance to God

A small group of faithful men, young and old, were united in silent submission to humbly seek God's deliverance and protection. They understood that His will was for our nation to freely follow Jesus Christ. The decisions that our First

Continental Congress made, based on the study of the Bible and prayer to our Christian God, would lead to events creating a document that would change the course of millions of lives centuries into the future, including yours.

The birth of the Declaration of Independence two years later, one of the most important documents in history, was derived from such acts of prayer. This simple, yet courageous show of loyalty to obey God instead of man would bring the greatest levels of Christian freedom ever seen, with unprecedented blessings to all who follow in agreement.

The first act of Congress occurred when our founding fathers humbled themselves and sought God. Walking in covenant gave them the bold confidence to petition Him for deliverance from tyranny as they laid the foundations for self-government built upon Jesus Christ. Yet, as we saw our nation's covenant begins much earlier, with the settlers consecrating our nation to God as the first act of America.

Our Covenant Christian Nation

The Bible and history show that following the Son of God results in God's safety, power, and prosperity for our nation. As Moses instructed Israel, America's pastors and political leaders John Hancock, George Washington, John Adams, and John Jay also taught to live pleasing God, which is to obey His government.

There is no authority, civil or religious—there can be no legitimate government but what is administered by this Holy

Ghost. There can be no salvation without it. All without it is rebellion and perdition, or in more orthodox words, damnation,[5] said John Adams

The Library of Congress says, *Congress... held that God bound himself in an agreement with a nation and its people. This agreement stipulated that they "should be prosperous or afflicted, according as their general Obedience or Disobedience thereto appears...*[6]

And government *was convinced... the 'public prosperity' of a society depended on the vitality of its [Christian] religion. Nothing less than a 'spirit of universal reformation among all ranks and degrees of our citizens,' Congress declared to all, would 'make us a holy, that so we may be a happy people.'*[6]

Motivated to make disciples, our founders taught all children the Bible and Christian prayer in schools. In covenant George Washington assured Delaware Indian chiefs, *I am glad you have brought three of the children of your principal chiefs to be educated with us... You do well to wish to learn... above all, the religion of Jesus Christ. These will make you a greater and happier people than you are. Congress will do everything they can to assist you in this wise intention.*[7]

The USA is more superior than a nation of Christians, for if one person is in covenant, God honors our covenant. The Supreme Court said, *This is a Christian nation.*[8]

Boldly the Pledge of Allegiance testifies that our country is a Christian Republic with the phrase, *to the Republic for which it stands, one nation under God.* Which God? The LORD.

The USA's God Is the LORD

Our forefathers making the LORD our God is significant, because He is the one true God. *I am the first, and I am the last; and beside me there is no God* (Isaiah 44:6 KJV).

Our founders knew of three remarkable Bible accounts of God's covenant mercy. These are found with Kings Asa and Josiah, and Moses (2 Chronicles 15 and 34, Exodus 32).

With riots, divisions, and terrorists, there is some similarity for us to King Asa's day when there was no peace... nation was destroyed of nation, and city of city (2 Chronicles 15:5-6). But Asa found hope that God was with Judah while they were with Him; and if they sought Him, He would be found. God would free them of the trouble. Asa knew the LORD was righteous and if they weren't with God, He wouldn't be with them (2 Chronicles 15:2).

King Josiah lived in a time where the Word of God was set aside and forgotten. He loved God, so to honor the LORD he commissioned the repairing of God's temple. Suddenly the Law of God was found in the recesses of the temple and the priests brought it to the king. For the first time in his life Josiah heard these words and saw the connection between the nation's sins and God's judgment. Seeing that God's judgment was on Judah, he tore his clothes in desperation and fear. He ordered the false gods to be destroyed and led the people to serve the LORD and turn from evil.

When Josiah inquired of God, he discovered their lives were in jeopardy for forsaking God and said, *great is the wrath of the LORD that is poured out upon us, because our fathers have not kept the word of the LORD* (2 Chronicles 34:21 KJV). So King Josiah and the people renewed covenant to live for the LORD and a great revival came.

We must have a tender heart of love for God and reaffirm covenant. Amazingly, revival came after evil King Manasseh forgot God. There is hope. God's favor returned when the people showed God they loved Him and *entered into a covenant to seek the LORD God of their fathers with all their heart and with all their soul* (2 Chronicles 15:12 KJV).

First Bible Truth for protection and blessings Psalm 33:12, 2 Cor. 6:16	Re-affirm Covenant: The LORD is the God of the USA and Americans are His people *Why? To get our nation in right relationship with God.*

The only way to be blessed is to make the one true God our God. *Blessed is the nation whose God is the LORD; and the people whom he hath chosen for his own inheritance* (Psalm 33:12 KJV). The opposite is true. The people who don't declare the LORD is the USA's God curse the nation.

The First Bible Truth to make the USA great again is to re-affirm covenant the USA's God is the LORD. This American breakthrough secret assures that God will make our nation great and restore His kind blessings to our lives, making Americans (those in covenant) God's special people. By doing this, we are in right relationship with God and are not His enemy. It is helpful to remember the Bible teaches the world is God's enemy (James 4:4).

Say the USA Is a Christian Nation

America is dedicated to God by many of the most mature Christians ever. Our journey to freedom is much like Israel's deliverance out of bondage in Egypt and their journey into the promised land. Our founders also found a promised land "to enjoy the liberties of the gospel".[4] What do the USA and Israel have in common? Both are covenant nations to the LORD from the start. Our God is a covenant God.

No other nation has the same covenant with Jesus Christ that the USA has with God. We are unique and our covenant must be faithfully protected.

Israel's covenant is through Abraham and continued with Moses. Other nations became Christian nations, but America made a covenant to God through Jesus Christ from the start.

Every Christian must know that our covenant is why God guards and blesses the USA. We give God everything and He gives us everything. He doesn't give His favored blessings to those not in covenant (1 Peter 2:9, Deuteronomy 26:18).

God wants a covenant for it defines who are His people. A covenant is holy and unbreakable. Having great wisdom, our founders understood that our nation could be God's people through the New Covenant of Jesus Christ, which is for whosoever believes and it is a "better covenant" than the Old Covenant (Hebrews 8:6 KJV).

A husband and wife making a family covenant to God is one example of the USA as a covenant Christian nation. We know God wants covenant nations as Israel proves.

Those who disagree are the people causing God's judgment, because to say America is no longer a Christian nation is a covenant breaking act. Consider Judah. Was the country no longer a covenant nation to the LORD when King Manasseh and the people did so much evil? At least one person was faithful to God. Thus when King Josiah took reign, the nation followed God.

That is where some people miss it. Are you no longer a Christian if you fall into sin? As long as you hold onto Jesus, which is holding onto covenant, you are a Christian. *For a just man falleth seven times, and riseth up again* (Proverbs 24:16 KJV).

Even though Judah killed their children and tolerated homosexual sin at times, the faithful remnant arose and repented, which resulted in magnificent revival. If King Josiah had said Judah (Israel) was not a covenant nation, God would have removed them, as He did later. But Josiah was part of the remnant who faithfully believed God.

Our founders saw others who didn't believe, but that didn't stop them. In the beginning just tens or hundreds of people claimed America for God. Look what their faith did!

It is unwise to listen to Obama and those outside of our covenant. Their words have no meaning. David never paid attention to uncircumcised Goliath. Abraham did not listen to the Sodomites. The devil is the one that tempts people to doubt the things of God. We must never betray God and country by giving up America's foundation on Jesus Christ.

What about unbelievers in the USA? God's law applies to believers and unbelievers. *One ordinance shall be both for you of the congregation, and also for the stranger that sojourneth with you* (Numbers 15:15 KJV). The believer sanctifies the unbeliever (1 Corinthians 7:14). By covenant Christian are in charge. As another proof the USA is a Christian nation, almost all political candidates say they are Christians, even if they aren't.

An amazing point is that 11% of all the Christians on the earth live in the USA.[7] This is higher than every other country. The USA has only 4.4% of the total population of the world. Those calling themselves Christians greatly outnumber all others in our nation. More than seven out of ten identify as Christians. There are few Hindus, 0.7%, and few Muslims, 0.9%.[8] The large majority chooses Christianity, even though not all have called on Jesus Christ to save their soul.

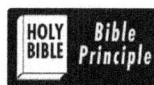

HOLY BIBLE *Bible Principle*

God rewards covenant acts of loyalty.

We must stop the sin of political correctness to not offend unbelievers who came to our Christian nation. Hiding the truth the USA is a Christian nation offends and angers God.

We combine God and country to make the USA holy. The Declaration of Independence, Pledge of Allegiance, and Constitution do this. We glorify the LORD in songs like *God Bless America, My Country 'Tis of Thee, America the Beautiful,* and our national anthem that says, *Praise the P'wer that has preserved and kept us... And this be our motto: "In God is our trust."*

Just as God and His mercy keeps your personal covenant with Him intact, He keeps the USA's covenant intact. God is faithful. I proclaim: *The LORD is the God of the USA and Americans are His people,* so I am in full covenant. I submit our country entirely to God continually. This is saying the USA is a Christian nation to all generations. Will you join me?

Today millions of Americans love God. By doing what our founders did, we will have a strong Christian nation. Will you and your church reclaim the USA for Jesus? Our founders were more mature Christians than those who state the USA isn't a Christian nation. They took our nation by spiritual force.

We need to remain faithful to God, for if no one holds fast to covenant, then Satan and evil people can destroy our country and harm millions of people. It is the devil saying that our founders weren't Christians but deists to ruin our lives.

Our founders' acts prove they are Christians. Remember, if our forefathers sinned in some area, God is more gracious than we are. God honors David who sinned but repented. He never said David wasn't a believer, but honors him.

Sadly, some Christians criticize our founders, even weak pastors are involved in this treason. But have those dishonoring our forefathers risked their life for the USA to break free from tyranny to follow God? Do they say America belongs to Jesus Christ? Have they put the Bible in schools?

Will they declare to our country their "abhorrence and detestation" of homosexual sin as George Washington did?[9] We are to hold fast to covenant and honor our founders.

Covenant Acts

Look at some of the USA's covenant acts that God blesses:
- The covenants (Jamestown Settlers, Pilgrims, Puritans...)
- The Revolution motto, "No king but King Jesus"
- George Washington reading the Holy Bible and praying in Jesus' name as the first act of Congress
- Teaching it is the duty of nations to serve God
- Americans declaring they obey God rather than man in the Declaration of Independence
- Singing "We trust in God: New England's God forever reigns" in the American Revolution song *Chester*
- The Constitution protecting our God-given rights
- All 50 states making Bible based laws for righteousness, such as outlawing sodomy and killing unborn children
- The Holy Bible and Christian Prayer in Schools for all children, Christian or non-Christian
- Government attending Christian churches in the Capital
- Our National Anthem saying, "In God is our trust"
- "This nation under God," affirmed Abraham Lincoln
- Our National Motto is "In God we trust"
- US currency saying, "In God we trust"
- Government *recognizes the Supreme Authority and Just Government of Almighty God,*[10] said Abraham Lincoln
- The National Day of Prayer, Christmas, and Thanksgiving supported by Federal law

- "One Nation Under God" in the Pledge of Allegiance
- All who agree, *Jesus Christ is Lord of the USA*

Re-affirming Covenant Is How to End Terrorism

We know how to stop losing the war on terror. Terrorism is defeated by: (1) Covenant acts that the LORD is the God of the USA and (2) Our nation obeying the Bible (Leviticus 26:14-16). To protect our loved ones, declare *Jesus Christ is Lord of the USA.*

The 7 Bible Truths are guaranteed by God to end terror, which has been a curse from our national sins. We are to proudly celebrate American culture of God and country. When we say the USA is a Christian nation, we ask God to protect His nation and He does.

Jesus Makes America Safe, Prosperous, and Blessed

As a nation, we have seen more of heaven on earth than those living in any other country. The USA is historically known for blessed lives, wisdom, godly behavior, and Christian freedom, because of these covenant acts. Americans have secure futures. No other nation compares to the USA.

What a glorious blessing it is to have the Holy Spirit fill our country when the people of this great nation draw near to God. As we abide in Christ and His Words abide in us, we dwell with God (John 15:7). Our lives and nation are filled with Christian love, wisdom, forgiveness, and truth. God's presence is seen in having the security and freedom we desire.

America has stood above all other nations in prosperity. Higher employment rates, better jobs, and the dollar having greater value come by our nation making Jesus our priority.[11,12] For many generations, there was no personal income tax. This is because most Christians earlier were bolder and called for righteousness, which results in blessings, such as keeping your whole paycheck (Matthew 6:33).

We have happier lives when the USA puts our Lord first. More people stay married with the Bible in society. Part of the reason comes from Christian encouragement to find God's answers to marriage issues, including forgiveness. Earlier generations found Biblical ways to work out family challenges and keep their marriage covenants.

Strong families were common earlier because people served God. More people married and broken homes were rare, with only 0.3 divorces or annulments per 1,000 people in the 1870's.[13] Just 3.8% of births were to unwed mothers in 1940, but now 40.2% of births are to unmarried women.[14]

Jesus gives us purpose in life, and living for Him helps children find God's plan for their lives. Public schools read the Bible and sought God with Christian prayer from 1607 to 1962. This produced people with integrity, reduced crime, and resulted in people more likely to go to heaven not hell.

Jesus Christ said our first responsibility is to love the LORD your God (Mark 12:30). For this reason, those who made our country raised American children to love and follow God. Public schools educated children with, *The love of God comprehends the love of all his attributes—the love of his justice in condemning and punishing sin—as well as of his mercy in forgiving and saving penitent sinners...* [15]

Children are better educated and have less troubles when taught the Bible in school, because the Holy Spirit fills their lives with wisdom, understanding, and knowledge (Proverbs 1). Our family and friends are more likely to go to heaven by trusting in Jesus for their salvation when the government promotes the Gospel as our founders did. Christians are honored and not persecuted. The whole nation is safer.

The USA has been blessed with national security from God, with peace for the people. The best security program is one that establishes a structure where we abide with God in our personal lives and as a nation as Psalm 91 assures.

HOLY BIBLE *Bible Principle*

Serving the LORD only keeps the USA safe from dictators and Shariah law.

Here the psalmist confidently trusts in God's perfect and complete protection from evil. He was pursued and persecuted, yet he found that no army, terrorist, or calamity can harm those who make God their habitation.

The blessings of heaven determine the difference between peace and war. The Kingdom of God frees us from oppression, Shariah law, godless world government, communism, socialism, and all non-Christian ways. The preeminent strategy of wicked leaders is to destroy trust in God. Tyranny is easy, if God is removed from the hearts and minds of the people. But faith in God always defeats tyrants.

Additional blessings that come by rallying together and defending Christianity as a nation are:

- Following Jesus Christ is what makes the USA one of God's greatest assets on earth
- Protecting Christians
- National sovereignty and unity
- Ridding our country of corruption
- The best leaders
- Freedom from a police state (i.e. the militarization of the police force, restricting free speech, martial law...)
- National security from God and peace for the people

Will You Choose the LORD for the USA's God?

We are a Christian Republic, with God as our sovereign. Then under God we the people are next sovereign. Americans do not believe in a ruling political class. Our forefathers say Jesus is sovereign above all government (Psalm 2).

John Hancock is one of the most respected men in our free country who risked his life for our Christian liberty. One could say he is the first modern American as he signed the Declaration of Independence first with the largest signature as president of the fearless Continental Congress. As governor, he publicly led the people with, *The great and most important Blessing, the Gospel of Jesus Christ... that all may bow to the scepter of our LORD JESUS CHRIST...*[16]

George Washington taught, *It is the duty of nations... to obey His will.*[17] Our second president, John Adams reminds us, *The Christian religion is, above all the religions...*[18] Some may be surprised to discover how strongly John Hancock, George Washington, John Adams, and our founders sought God and relied on Him for our nation. Many don't know these truths about combining God and country because of a long-term and subtle strategy by the father of lies to remove Christianity from our nation's children.

Without young people knowing the truth of our Christian nation, they would live under a covenant that is broken, which means having much less; it could also be suffering in communism or the removal of the nation. So, we must help every child know the amazing American story.

Will you join covenant by agreeing the USA's God is the one true God? This lets Him know that you and the USA are on His side, which means safety, strength, liberty, and the defeat of our enemies. Just reject all other gods, since they cause harm, and declare, *The LORD is my God and I am His.*

Since the LORD is our God and He is good, we thank, praise, and worship Him. This is part of having the LORD be our God. Everyday we magnify Him by saying things like, "I and the USA exalt You LORD." He is worthy!

As we glorify Him, He defeats our enemies (2 Chronicles 20). That is why agreeing that the USA serves the true God gives us national security. For our protection, all churches should hold services re-affirming the USA serves the LORD.

If you read the *Harbinger* book, you probably wanted to know what to do next. These powerful *7 Bible Truths* are the solution to the *Harbinger*, which is from the Isaiah 9:10

analogy of the bricks falling and the sycamore tree being cut down. God's answer for America's future is found on another tree—the more significant tree at Calvary. Four verses before we find God's remedy of Jesus Christ, *the government shall be upon His shoulder* (Isaiah 9:6); the cross at Calvary gives us mercy and grace. Everything is restored by Jesus.

The first step to do this important work and to make the USA great again is deciding to serve the one true God. All other gods are to be seen as harmful to us. Those who won't renounce strange gods are the ones who endanger the country. But, all who follow the LORD make the USA great.

Next, we learn valuable, true American secrets.

✝ Prayer

Father, You, LORD, are the God of the USA
and Americans are Your people.
In Jesus' name. Amen.

✓ Reflection Questions

1. *Christians serve a different God than other people. Explain why the LORD is the one true God.*
2. *Why does God's favor come by renouncing other gods?*
3. *Read Psalm 33:12. Will you publicly say the LORD is the God of the USA? Why?*
4. *How could the faith of only a few first Christian settlers make the greatest Christian nation ever?*

3

American Secrets for Safe and Blessed Lives

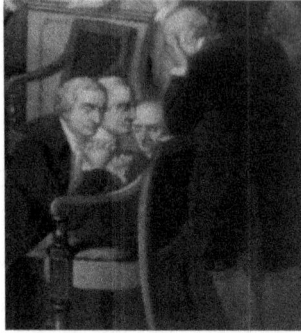

The founding fathers seeking God in Congress.
John Jay, first Chief Justice, is second from left.

"The secret of the LORD is with them that fear him; and he will shew them his covenant." KJV
Psalm 25:14

Americans have stood far above all other nations with God's protection, freedom, and abundance. So, let's answer: What are the next things our founders did to attain these special blessings? How can we do the same?

There are *American Secrets* that honor God as first place in everything for our nation. They are a key foundation for the *7 Bible Truths* and are core beliefs of the famed pastors and Christians who founded America. Much of the corruption has been because these mature Christian beliefs have been missing from many churches, who only teach basic Christianity, which does not produce America.

42

Following these secrets makes our churches great again and exceptional congregations make the USA great.

---

7 American Secrets †▬▬

Christian Religious Liberty
Insist the USA serves the LORD only.
Matthew 4:10 & 12:30, Galatians 5:1

One Nation Under God
The USA is a covenant Christian nation.
Psalm 33:12, Jamestown Settlers, Pilgrims...

God-given Rights
Demand life, liberty, the pursuit of happiness, conscience and property. Genesis 1:27, Lev. 25:10

Basic Christianity
Christ died for our sins, was buried, rose again...
1 Corinthians 15:3-8, Mark 12:30-31

Righteousness Exalts the USA
No false gods, be pro-life, traditional marriage only... Proverbs 14:34

Jesus Christ Leads the Government
It is the duty of nations to obey God.
Isaiah 9:6 & 33:22

Christian Disciple Making As a Nation
The Bible in schools, chaplains pray in Jesus' name... as Jesus and our founders teach.
Matthew 28:19-20

These are 7 beliefs of true American pastors. Churches must teach these beliefs so the USA is safe and blessed. Political leaders are to advance the Kingdom of God.

Secret 1: Insist to Have Christian Religious Liberty

Our founders understood God's First Commandment is to love the LORD. So, they made freedom to serve Jesus Christ the USA's number one priority. Our nation and Israel have in common because both demanded to serve the LORD as a country, even when tyrants, such as King George and Pharaoh, said no.

God abundantly rewarded our founders by freeing the USA from England. This is like how God freed Israel from slavery. If you want oppression removed, then have faith, for

43

God is against tyranny. He fought for His people, undoing the Egyptian's chariot wheels in the Red Sea (Exodus 14:25). Since God is against tyranny, Christians also oppose it.

The USA and Israel both have the greatest political leaders in history, other than Jesus Christ who is King of kings. God defines a leader as a just man *ruling in the fear of God* (2 Samuel 23:3 KJV). Among Israel's leaders are Moses and kings Asa and Josiah who led people to God. Our founders mentioned in this book are many of America's premiere leaders, including the pastors who taught them.

A well known preacher, Declaration signer, and a ratifier of the Constitution, John Witherspoon, said, *Whoever is an avowed enemy of God, I scruple not to call him an enemy to his country.*[1] The colonial clergy *were men not only of eminent piety... but were ardent lovers of liberty,*[2] shared historian Benjamin Morris. Deep in our hearts and churches is pure love for God. America's first secret is insisting the USA has Christian religious liberty to serve the LORD.

We must only stand up for Christian religious liberty to serve the LORD, not religious liberty of false gods. The reason is so we don't provoke God (2 Chronicles 34:25). Our Christian founders typically used the word "religion" to mean Christianity, since the King James Version of the Bible does this (James 1:26-27). When we read our founding fathers saying "religious liberty," they often mean "Christian liberty". To prove this, they put the Bible in schools, not other beliefs.

That is why the media, politicians, ministers, and those who say "freedom of all religions" put the nation in great risk.

To help other gods is dangerous. If Moses had said, "Israel must have liberty for Baal and also the LORD," God could have killed Moses for forsaking Him (Exodus 32). When Aaron sinned with the molten calf, Moses reminds us, *the LORD was very angry with Aaron to have destroyed him* (Deuteronomy 9:20 KJV). God is holy. As our Creator and Judge, He calls the USA to worship Him only, not strange gods. It is a covenant breaking act to help false religions. If you have aided other gods, confess this sin and be forgiven. Then, be like our founders and stand up for Christian liberty, not "freedom of all religions".

Secret 2: The USA Is a Covenant Christian Nation

We have seen our founders' covenant with the LORD. This is the second American secret. So let's look at some other aspects about this.

Abraham Lincoln along with our founders believed that our nation would be blessed as long as we maintained our relationship with Jesus. As president, Lincoln proclaimed, *Recognize the sublime truth, announced in the Holy Scriptures and proven by all history, that those nations only are blessed whose God is the Lord.*[4] He also shared, *It is the duty of nations as well as of men, to own their dependence upon the overruling power of God.*[4]

HOLY BIBLE *Bible Principle*

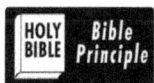

You are created in the image of God and hold a noble rank in creation.

Our country became a weak Christian nation by taking the Bible and Christian prayer out of schools, but the USA is a Christian nation always by covenant. Yet, we are getting stronger again. Thanks to God, I see great revival with people.

Some go so far as to think the USA is Babylon. They speculate everything is over, but that is not true. We fix all our problems by teaching the powerful *7 Bible Truths* and these 7 American secrets. Our work is very important since lives are at stake. As the remnant of true American believers we have faith that God will help us.

Secret 3: Demand Our God-given Rights

Your rights come from God, not man (Acts 5:29). The Declaration of Independence says, *all men are endowed by their Creator with certain unalienable rights, among these are life, liberty, and the pursuit of happiness.* This also gives you the right of property and conscience. No one can take away our rights because God gives our rights, not man or government (Acts 5:29).

America's third secret to safe and blessed lives is to demand our God-given rights, since man is made in the image of God (Genesis 1:27). John Adams said to pastors, *Let us hear the dignity of his nature, and the noble rank he holds among the works of God—that consenting to [tyranny] slavery is a sacrilegious breach of trust, as offensive in the sight of God as it is derogatory from our own honor or interest or happiness—and that God Almighty has promulgated from heaven liberty, peace, and good-will to man!*[5]

Your unalienable rights are to live for God, and include:

- **Life:** You have the right to life in all you do, beginning at conception. In Jesus is life, so this right is to follow Him. The Bible says, *In Him was life; and the life was the light of men* (John 1:4 KJV). "Life is the immediate gift of God, a right inherent by Nature [God's creation] in every individual and it begins in contemplation of law as soon as an infant is able to stir in the mother's womb" and "consists in the free use, enjoyment, and disposal of every man's acquisitions, without any control or diminution,"[6] explained scholar Sir William Blackstone.

- **Liberty:** Your right of liberty includes freedom to live your life for God as a Christian, not to live in sin. Jesus is the Author of Liberty and only He makes you free. Personal liberty "consists in the power of removing one's person to any place whatsoever without restraint, unless by due course of law," said Blackstone.[7] Americans reject tyranny because tyrants oppose God.

- **The Pursuit of happiness:** Your right to the pursuit of happiness is to do God's will because you are created in such a way that you can only be happy doing God's will. Psalm 144:15 says, "happy is that people, whose God is the LORD. The law of nature (the will of God) forbids doing things that are against another person's pursuit of happiness. Jesus commanded, *Thou shalt love thy neighbour as thyself* (Mark 12:31).

- **Property:** You have the right to property. This includes using your property to glorify God. *The earth is the*

LORD's, and the fullness thereof (Psalm 24:1 KJV). A person's right of private property "consists in the free use, enjoyment, and disposal of all his acquisitions, without any control or diminution, save only by the [Christian] laws of the land," explained Blackstone.[8]

- **Conscience:** Your right of conscience is the duty to obey your conscience before God in holiness (Acts 5:29). The Bible teaches that no one can force you to sin. A person who tries to force you to sin is evil.

The LORD gives us God-given rights to be holy, He does not give us rights to sin. This means that "homosexual, rights," "abortion rights" and other sins are Satan-given rights. To avoid God' wrath, our founders opposed rights to sin.

Unalienable Rights Are a Non-negotiable

Boldly the "father of the Revolution," Samuel Adams, reminds us of our sacred duty to keep our rights, *The right to freedom being the gift of God Almighty...*[9] We should think like our founders. Abiding in Christ as free men and making disciples is higher living than just getting saved.

We need every pastor to teach our God-given rights. *The clergy in all the colonies were bold and frequent in their pulpit enunciations of the great principles of civil and [Christian] religious liberty and in rebuking despotism and the evils of the day,* explained Robert Morris.[10]

Secret 4: Teach Basic Christianity

Our founders loved God with all their heart; they passionately believed and taught the Holy Bible. Now we must unite the USA in Christ. As Christians of different denominations, we agree on the following core beliefs of the Gospel of Jesus Christ:

- **God** - God eternally exists in three Persons as Father, Son, and Holy Spirit. He is the one true God (Matthew 28:19, Isaiah 43:10-11, John 8:58).
- **God's Word is infallible** - The Holy Bible is our final authority in all matters of faith and practice (2 Timothy 3:16-17, 2 Peter 1:21, 1 Thessalonians 2:13).
- **The fall of man and salvation through Jesus Christ** - All have sinned, come short of the glory of God, and face the judgment of God. Each person individually is to call on Jesus Christ to be saved, for by grace we are saved through faith. Jesus Christ was born of a virgin and lived a perfect sinless life; He is the Lamb of God who takes away the sin of the world and died on the cross, shedding His blood for our sins. He was buried, rose from the dead, and sits at the right hand of God (Romans 3:23 & 6:23, John 1:29 & 3:16, Ephesians 2:8-9, Matthew 1:23, Hebrews 7:26, Luke 22:20, 1 Corinthians 15:4, Mark 16:19).
- **God commands us to love Him and to love one another** - The First Commandment is to *love the Lord thy God with all thy heart, and with all thy soul, and with all thy mind, and with all thy strength: this is the*

49

first commandment. The Second Commandment is *to love thy neighbour as thyself* (Mark 12:30-31 KJV).

- **Christians are to live holy lives** - God gives us the Holy Spirit so we can glorify Him in all we do (Romans 8:13-14, Galatians 5:22-23).

Secret 5: Teach Righteousness Exalts the USA

Wanting our nation to glorify God, both the colonial and American Revolution pastors taught, *Righteousness exalteth a nation: but sin is a reproach to any people* (Proverbs 14:34 KJV). God is righteous; He is pro-life and for sexual purity of one man and one woman in a lifetime marriage.

Righteousness is the fifth secret to America's safety and blessings. This is to:

1) Serve the LORD only—not any other gods
2) Daily read the Holy Bible and have Christian prayer in schools and all government
3) Be pro-life
4) Have traditional marriage only
5) Other holy ways from the Bible

Secret 6: Jesus Christ Leads the Government

The purpose of government is to serve Jesus (Isaiah 9:6). That is why the Declaration of Independence says we have God-given unalienable rights and "to secure these rights, governments are instituted among men". The sixth secret to security and favor is for government, schools, courts, police forces, and the military to have their objective to glorify God.

Some think that church and state are to be kept separate, but the opposite is the truth. Our founders kept the state out of the church *not* the church out of the state. The water is to be out of the boat, but the boat is in the water.

The real question is, "Does God require the USA to obey Him?" He says, *If we deny Him, He also will deny us* (2 Timothy 2:12 KJV). The First Commandment is to love God, so the devil is behind the lie of separation of church and state (Mark 12:30). Freedom and abundance came to the USA and Israel by serving God.

The USA Honors Christians

Joseph Story was appointed to the Supreme Court in 1811 by James Madison and wrote our Constitution's first extensive commentary; **Justice Joseph Story explained the First Amendment is for Christianity.** The First Amendment is not to approve of non-Christian beliefs as some in error say today. Law students studied Story's popular "Commentaries on the Constitution" from 1833 to 1905. It explains:

> *The real object of the [First] Amendment was, not to countenance [approve], much less to advance Mohammedanism, or Judaism, or infidelity [secularism], by prostrating Christianity, but to exclude all rivalry among Christian sects, and to prevent any national ecclesiastical establishment*

51

[denomination], which should give to an hierarchy the exclusive patronage of the national government.[11]

In 1833 Chief Justice John Marshall affirmed Story's work as "an accurate commentary on our Constitution, formed in the spirit of the original text" that all statesmen should read.[12] The media, judges, and schools have lied about the First Amendment to use it against Christians by saying, "the Christian activity is a violation of church and state".

HOLY BIBLE	*Bible Principle*

The First Amendment prohibits laws against Christians as the First Commandment is to love the LORD.

Our founders prayed in Jesus' name, read the Bible in government, and wrote the Constitution. Laws against Christians and our conscience are illegal. **The First Amendment means:**

Congress [because its rights are limited] shall make no law respecting an establishment of [one Christian denomination] religion, or prohibiting the free exercise [of Christianity] thereof...

Christians wrote our Christian Constitution for Christians. It: (1) Begins with "blessings;" (2) Restricts Congress from making a law prohibiting the free exercise of Christianity in the First Amendment; (3) Includes "Sundays excepted" to honor the Lord in Article 1, Section 7; (4) Ends with "in the Year of our Lord" affirming Jesus Christ is Lord of the USA; and (5) Has Bible principles throughout. It is based on our Christian Declaration of Independence.

By our form of government, the Christian religion is the established religion; and all sects and denominations of Christians are placed upon the same equal footing, and are equally entitled to protection in their religious liberty,[13] said Justice Samuel Chase in the Maryland case Runkel v. Winemiller. George Washington appointed Chase to the Supreme Court.

The Bible tells us that Christians are the ones who cause God's favor to the USA, not unbelievers. That is why our founders taught school children, *Almost all civil liberty... owes its origin to the principles of the Christian religion. Men began to understand their natural rights, as soon as the reformation from popery began to dawn in the sixteenth century... to this we owe our free constitutions of government.*[14]

Secret 7: Christian Disciple Making in Government

Both the USA and Israel taught God's Word to the people because God asks for and blesses the government making disciples. This is America's seventh secret to have God's protection, freedom, and prosperity. We are not a state run church, but government supports Christian disciple making.

Our founding fathers show us that all Christian denominations run the government with one focus to advance the Christian faith. God wants the church in charge not sinners. God's will is that the church is in the driver's seat. But, the devil runs the parts not submitted to God.

To have Christianity in schools and for chaplains to pray in Jesus' name as our founders did, the church must want government to glorify God. Our forefathers made disciples by forbidding homosexual and other sins in government. Thomas Jefferson, James Madison, and Americans had Christian church in the Capitol.[15]

America Is Above All Nations

God's secrets of America reveal key reasons why He favors the USA. The *7 Bible Truths* and these secrets, which are part of the first Bible Truth, are what make Americanism.

Next, we learn how to find God and to have His help to make our lives and nation extraordinary.

✝ Prayer

Father, the USA exalts Jesus Christ.
Give every Christian boldness to demand to
have Christian religious liberty.
In Jesus' name. Amen.

✓ Reflection Questions

1. *How does righteousness exalt a nation? Explain.*
2. *Why does saying "freedom of all religions" anger God?*
3. *Explain each of your God-given rights.*

4

Second Truth—Seek and Find God

George Washington praying to the LORD God.

"They entered into a covenant to seek the LORD God
of their fathers with all their heart and with all their soul;"
2 Chronicles 15:12 KJV

George Washington kneels in desperation searching for answers. As commander in chief, all he could do at this point was seek the true Commander in Chief, our Lord. His men were sick, hungry, and cold. He had sought help earnestly from men, but it wasn't enough. So as he often did, he knelt to seek God's help at Valley Forge.

Seeking God Gives His Help and Answers

What is the next timely step to deliver us from our troubles, including avoiding an economic collapse, preventing wars, and fixing political problems? *The Second Bible Truth is seeking God with all our heart and all our soul means we find Him and have His help. We go from living in risk to finding God's wisdom and mighty deliverance.*

Second Bible Truth for protection and blessings 2 Chron. 15:12, Matt. 7:7	Seek God with all your heart and all your soul
	Why? To find God and His help.

Seeking God is the only way to do great things. We seek God so we do His will. If we don't seek God, then we do mediocre and sinful things. To seek God is to wholeheartedly look for Him, to know His will, and to find His help about fixing our nation's problems. Finding God's answer is knowing how to save our nation, instead of having false hope.

When Judah humbled themselves to make covenant in Asa's time, the people were happy to seek God and end their problems. *Judah rejoiced at the oath: for they had sworn with all their heart, and sought Him with their whole desire; and He was found of them: and the LORD gave them rest round about* (2 Chronicles 15:15 KJV). Judah was not destroyed in Josiah's life because God saw Josiah humble himself (2 Kings 22:19).

There is much to learn and gain by seeking God. Jesus promises, *Ask, and it shall be given you; seek, and ye shall find; knock, and it shall be opened unto you* (Matthew 7:7 KJV).

To put God first can be to not answer the phone or read our text messages until we have found Him. Moses often "fell upon his face" to seek God when in need and He immediately answered him. With all the sins in the USA, our whole nation should fall on our faces and seek God for immediate deliverance. Like Moses, we are to seek God with a deep hunger and as one who wants to find Him (Numbers 16:22).

God Rewards You for Seeking Him

We are to seek God for our personal lives to be right with Him. He wants us to walk with Him and find His counsel and miraculous help in all that we do.

As a personal example, one time as I sought God for His immediate direction in my life, I wrestled with decisions that would impact my future. I put all things aside to find God's help. Instead of pursuing doors I thought would be best, I sought God until He opened doors for me. I prayed daily to do God's will for my life and He revealed to me which doors to go through. As a result, a situation that I previously saw as insurmountable was now overcome.

You have confidence that God hears you, for every Christian is accepted with Him. By shedding His blood for you on the cross, Jesus makes you holy, without blemish, blameless, and above reproach, no matter what your sins have been. He presents you faultless with exceeding joy (Ephesians 1:6 & 5:22, Colossians 1:22, Jude 1:24, 1 John 1:7).

So have faith that your prayers are answered when you ask according to God's Word. When you ask God for His help, He lovingly helps you with His hand for your needs.

God is interested in each of us. He wants us to fellowship with Him, so He kindly invites us to know Him. David said, *Thy face, LORD, will I seek* (Psalm 27:8 KJV). This is knowing

God for who He is and not just for what He can do for us. This is another level of seeking God. We are created to worship God in reverence and to enjoy Him as our best friend.

He answers us when we pray in faith. He says, *Delight thyself also in the LORD; and he shall give thee the desires of thine heart* (Psalm 37:4 KJV). When you seek God:

- **You find God:** *Thou shalt find him, if thou seek him with all thy heart and with all thy soul.* (Deut. 4:29 KJV)
- **The LORD helps you:** *For You, LORD, have not forsaken those who seek You.* (Psalm 9:10 KJV)
- **God rewards you:** *But without faith it is impossible to please Him, for he who comes to God must believe that He is, and that He is a rewarder of those who diligently seek Him.* (Hebrews 11:6 KJV)
- **You prosper:** *As long as he sought the LORD, God made him to prosper.* (2 Chronicles 26:5 KJV)
- **You have all you need:** *They that seek the LORD shall not want any good thing.* (Psalm 34:10 KJV)
- **You do God's work:** *Now set your heart and your soul to seek the LORD your God; arise therefore, and build.* (2 Chronicles 12:14 KJV)
- **You have life:** *Your heart shall live* that seek God.* (Psalm 69:32 KJV) *The word "live" means to have life, live prosperously, and to be restored to health.
- **You avoid evil:** *He did evil, because he prepared not his heart to seek the LORD.* (2 Chronicles 12:14 KJV)
- **You understand all things:** *They that seek the LORD understand all things.* (Proverbs 28:5 KJV)

How to Find God in Your Personal Life

Here are five Biblical principles to help find God. First, each of us must make the decision to live following God. The Bible says, *Submit yourselves therefore to God. Resist the devil, and he will flee from you* (James 4:7 KJV). Remove anything unholy in your life. Put off ungodly conversations, thoughts, shows, art, and anything that displeases God. Instead, seek the things above where Christ is seated (Colossians 3:1-3). The Holy Spirit gives you self control, so think thoughts of love for God and others. Then resist the devil. A good prayer is, *Father, You are holy. I want to be holy. Fill me with Your Holy Spirit so my life glorifies You. In Jesus' name. Amen.*

Second, pray God's Word. Jesus promises that if we abide in Him and His words abide in us, we shall ask what we will and it shall be done unto us (John 15:7).

The third thing to do is to have faith that God will answer you. Christians walk by faith, not by sight (2 Corinthians 5:7). To live by faith is to live by God's Word. We can pray, *Father, great is Your faithfulness. I walk by Your Word. Thank You for answering me. In Jesus' name. Amen.*

A secret that God graciously revealed to me is to never stop seeking Him until I find Him, whether it takes a moment or two hours. God is faithful to answer us when we believe that He will help us right now. If we expect God's immediate help, we see answers and miracles quickly (Mark 11:23-24).

Fourth, seek God continually, not just when in trouble. God promises, *He that dwells in the secret place of the Most High shall abide under the shadow of the Almighty* (Psalm

91:1). *Evening, and morning, and at noon, will I pray, and cry aloud: and He shall hear my voice* (Psalm 55:17 KJV).

Fifth, let God know that you are willing to do His will. When you let go of your will, you can find God's will. God says, *I have found David... a man after Mine own heart, which shall fulfill all My will* (Acts 13:22 KJV). These Biblical points help all your prayers be answered, even immediately.

So I can draw near to God quickly and have deeper fellowship with Him, in the morning, after telling God I love Him and blessing Him, I pray the four steps of 2 Chronicles 7:14. *Father, I humble myself, pray, seek Your face, and turn from my wicked ways. In Jesus' name. Amen.*

When you make a decision, seek God first. He will lead you. If you don't know what to do, you can pray as a commitment prayer Proverbs 3:5-6. *Father, I trust in You with all my heart regarding ___. I lean not on my own understanding about this. I acknowledge You in this, and I thank You for directing my paths. In Jesus' name. Amen.*

Anything we seek God's will for can be placed in that blank line. If you are seeking God about where to serve Him, You would insert, "the perfect place You have for me to serve You," in the blank line. God will direct your steps since this is His promise.

> **HOLY BIBLE** *Bible Principle*
>
> *You find God when you seek Him with all your heart and all your soul.*

Jesus continually sought God to know His will, always finding and doing the Father's will. Jesus did this when He had to lay down His life for us at Calvary. Since Jesus is also a man, He didn't want to feel the immense suffering of the cross

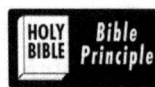

because He would be scourged, mocked, and painfully crucified for our sins.

With fear and great depression, knowing how much He would suffer for us to be forgiven of our sins, He fell down in Gethsemane and asked God if there was another way to save you and me. Since there was no other way, Jesus arose with courage and endured the cross for us. Hopefully you realize that "nothing could stop Jesus from loving you," as I say in my sermon, "Jesus Loved You on the Cross."

A popular hymn, "Sweet Hour of Prayer," encourages us to spend time with God in prayer, *That calls me from a world of care, and bids me at my Father's throne. Make all my wants and wishes known...* Prayer strengthens your life.

If you need God's peace, His power, the right words to comfort someone, or assistance with what you are doing, just ask Him. He promises to *supply all your need according to His riches in glory by Christ Jesus* (Philippians 4:19 KJV).

One day I had a three hundred mile drive to make, but because of my busy schedule at USA Christian Church I could not leave until 8 p.m. After driving thirty minutes I was tired and I didn't think I could go further. But I prayed in faith for God to help me and to safely get me to my destination, expecting Him to answer me immediately. Miraculously in just minutes I felt God's strength and grace. I was awake and a five hour drive seemed like it was only two hours!

How to Seek God for the USA

Our nation seeking God is especially important. Let's look at a couple examples from Scripture.

Moses knew God because He sought God. Recall, when Israel turned to the molten calf and forsook the LORD, God saw this sin as a covenant breaking act. He said to Moses, *let me alone, that my wrath may wax hot against them, and that I may consume them* (Exodus 32:10 KJV). However, God allowed Moses to remind Him of covenant with Israel. Then Moses separated the people by finding out who loved God and who didn't by asking: Who is on the LORD'S side? (Exodus 32:10-26 KJV). If Moses had not sought God, all the people might have died.

When Israel suffered a famine, King David sought God and learned what sin caused judgment. *The LORD answered, It is for Saul, and for his bloody house, because he slew the Gibeonites* (2 Samuel 21:1 KJV). The Gibeonites lived in Israel's promised land and were to be destroyed. But they lied to Israel and Israel made a treaty because they didn't seek God (Joshua 9). Then, when Saul went against Joshua's words, God judged them. But David found the answer to stop judgment!

I hope that you are optimistic because doing these *Bible Truths* will bring back jobs for Americans and give us peace not war. Following God's blueprint will save millions of souls, heal marriages, free our nation from communist threats, and have Christians honored in schools and at work again.

To help our nation seek the LORD, here are some questions that we and our churches can prayerfully ask:

- Will this act bring God's blessings or judgment?
- Does this decision bring Americans closer to God?
- How can the USA's sins be forgiven?
- Why does God forbid America to have other gods?
- If we do this will more go to Heaven or hell?

- What qualifications does God have for leaders?
- How does the Bible say to drain the swamp of political corruption?
- Will this choice make us more heavenly or worldly?
- What national sins can we repent of?

God has the answers we are searching for. By faith we believe that God is removing everything against Him from the USA and young Americans will live as faithful Christians. God will reward our work (2 Chronicles 15:7).

Those Not Seeking God Lack Wisdom

Even as we desire God, there may still be those who don't renounce strange gods or their pursuit of the world, which perpetuates God's wrath. King Asa realized this Scriptural revelation. The Old Testament says, *whosoever would not seek the LORD God of Israel should be put to death, whether small or great, whether man or woman* (2 Chronicles 15:13 KJV). Moses and King Josiah also put to death those who wouldn't follow God (Exodus 32:26-28, 2 Kings 23:4-25). **For us, we don't kill people, but we "turn away" from those responsible for our nation's judgment** (2 Timothy 3:5).

Are there ungodly TV programs, anti-Christian news stations, or sinful friends that God wants you to turn away from? They are interested in the world instead of God, so we don't gain any benefit by listening to them. While we share in love to those living in darkness that Jesus died on the cross to forgive our sins, the Bible teaches that we are to turn away from sinful things.

Our founders only appointed Christian chaplains to seek God. That is why the House Judiciary Committee, *resolved, that the daily sessions of this body be opened with prayer and that... the [Christian] ministers of the Gospel... are hereby requested to attend and alternately perform this solemn duty.*[1]

God is with those who are with Him, so Congress in 1777 declared, *That it may please GOD, through the Merits of Jesus Christ... to afford his Blessing on the Governments of these States... to prosper the Means of [Christian] Religion for the promotion and enlargement of that Kingdom which consists 'in Righteousness, Peace and Joy in the Holy Ghost.*[2]

Since the answer to be free of high taxes and riots is to seek and obey God as a nation, pray to the LORD only. This makes the USA safe and strong (2 Kings 17:15-20, Deuteronomy 28:29, Ezekiel 16:37).

Seeking God Puts You on God's Side

George Washington and his men made it through that difficult winter in Valley Forge defending our freedom because he humbled himself before the true Commander in Chief and found Him. God faithfully answered his prayer. When spring arrived, although the army was weakened, they were able to claim a resounding victory! Eventually God gave us complete victory and independence since Americans kept seeking Him with all their heart and soul.

Seeking God looks like George Washington pleading for God's help to defeat a stronger army. It looks like King Josiah tearing his clothes and weeping when he hears God's words and his eyes open, seeing the sins of the people. It looks like

American pastors praying in Jesus' name for government, schools, courts, and the military.

It also looks like those joining in the nationwide prayer and fasting on Wednesdays to heal our land that I am hosting,5 to have a Christian government, and our nation repenting of everything against Jesus Christ (Luke 11:2, 1 John 3:8).

Our founders trusted in God and He kept the USA safe from enemies, foreign and domestic. The Bible says, Put not your trust in princes, nor in the son of man, in whom there is no help and except the LORD keep the city, the watchman wakes but in vain (Psalm 146:3 KJV, Psalm 127:1).

Now, it is our turn to be faithfully known for praying, In God We Trust. The USA's hope is God! We are to keep seeking God until we find Him.

If you haven't been seeking Him, I encourage you to start now. He wants to hear from you. His grace welcomes you!

Will you turn to God with all your heart and soul? If so, you are on His side. Then you can say, *The LORD is on my side; I will not fear: what can man do unto me?* (Psalm 118:6 KJV). Have faith! He always rewards the USA for seeking Him. Victory and miracles happen!

The next *Bible Truth* reveals how to do God's will.

✝ Prayer

Here is a prayer to seek God together as a nation:

Father,

Americans love You—You are the USA's God and we are Your people. With all our heart and soul, we seek You to:

65

- *Mercifully end Your judgment.*
- *Lead our country. The USA submits to You.*
- *Give us Christian leaders who fear You for school boards, city, state, and federal government.*
- *Lead Americans not into temptation. Deliver the USA from evil (everything against You).*
- *Teach us if __ will make our nation holy, or unholy.*
- *Show Americans what Your Word says about __.*
- *We trust in You to protect the USA from all enemies foreign and domestic.*

Americans thank and praise You.

In Jesus' name. Amen.

✝ Reflection Questions

1. *Why does seeking God protect your life? Explain.*
2. *How often do you seek God in the decisions you make?*
3. *In what ways can you be like King Asa and King Josiah in seeking God with all your heart and all your soul? What are some things you will do?*
4. *How can your church seek God for the USA? In what ways? How often?*

5

Third Truth—Live the Bible Way

"To keep His commandments... with all his heart, and with all his soul, to perform the words of the covenant which are written in this book."
2 Chronicles 34:31 KJV

Jesus Christ is the Word of God. This is an important reason why we stand in awe of God's Word. God says, *In the beginning was the Word, and the Word was with God, and the Word was God* and *His name is called The Word of God* (John 1:1, Revelation 19:13 KJV).

When King Josiah and Judah found the Word of God that their fathers lost, the people followed God. They *made a covenant before the LORD, to walk after the LORD, and to keep his commandments...* (2 Chronicles 34:31 KJV). Living for God saved their lives. Like Judah found the book of the law, we are learning from the Word of God these *7 Bible Truths* that safeguard our lives and homes.

The LORD Is Our Lawgiver

The Third Bible Truth to make the USA great is obedience to the Word of God assures that God will protect our lives and nation, gives us wisdom, and makes the economy strong. Safety comes by obeying God's Word. This is because we do His will. To obey God goes with the *Second Bible Truth* to seek and find Him, since part of seeking Him is to learn what He says. This is living the Bible way. To love God is to do what He says and this make the nation remarkable. We do the greatest work possible by obeying the Bible.

Third Bible Truth for protection and blessings Luke 6:47-49, 2 Chron. 34:31	Obey the Holy Bible with all your heart and all your soul Why? To do God's will.

Both our personal and nation's relationship with God is by His Word. To find God's will, pray: *What does the Bible say about this?* Then find in Scripture what a Christian is to do. We are on God's side when we keep His Word (John 15:14).

Who makes our laws? The Bible says, *the LORD is our lawgiver* (Isaiah 33:22 KJV). To have justice, we must affirm the Bible is God's revealed law. It is our duty to obey our Creator or we face consequences. *The doctrines thus delivered we call the revealed or divine law, and they are to be found only in the Holy Scriptures,*[1] taught legal scholar Sir William Blackstone.

The Bible Is the Secret to Remarkable Blessings

Here are seven blessings that God's Word gives you personally. First, you grow closer to God by knowing His Word (Psalm 119). Second, the Word of God gives you life (Matthew 4:4). The third important benefit is having what you ask of God, since you ask according to His will (1 John 5:15, John 15:7).

Wisdom is the fourth amazing blessing (Proverbs 1). The fifth benefit is keeping God's Word gives you health (Exodus 15:26, Proverbs 4:20-22). The sixth benefit is having a true Christian home serving God (Joshua 24:15). The seventh blessing is strong faith, for *faith cometh by hearing, and hearing by the word of God* (Romans 10:17 KJV).

God gives us incomparable blessings when we observe and do what He says. God gave the USA the Deuteronomy 28 blessings before and He wants to do this now. He set America high above all nations, made the USA blessed in the city and in the field, and blessed American children, produce, and animals. He lovingly blessed the USA coming and going. He defeated America's enemies, commanded the blessing in all we do, and set Americans as a holy people to Himself.

But there is more... God made Americans plenteous in everything, prospered the USA financially—by lending to others not borrowing, and made us the head not the tail. Keeping God's Word makes the USA great.

Your greatest blessings also come from the Bible. He tells you how to live the best way possible now and to be rewarded in Heaven.

What Makes the Bible the #1 Best Seller?

Why did God give us the Word of God? He preserves His Word to all generations so we can know Him and walk with Him as our lawgiver, live in happiness, and be safe from harm. We learn the eternal mind and counsel of God when we read God's Word. The Bible is unique as it does not have human origin and it is the absolute final authority for us and our nation. That is why the Holy Bible is the top selling book in history and quoted by our respected founders.

God says to love one another, be honest, for families to stay together, forgive one another, believe that He will provide for us, live righteously, and how to be saved from the wrath to come. Is there anything unjust in the Bible?

My most valuable possession is my Bible. By God's Word, I know God and have everything I need. Here are ten keys why the Bible is of greater worth than every other book:

- **The Holy Bible is God's Word** from Genesis to Revelation - *All Scripture is given by inspiration of God (2 Timothy 3:16 KJV); For the prophecy came not in old time by the will of man: but holy men of God spake as they were moved by the Holy Ghost (2 Peter 1:21 KJV).*
- **The Word of God cannot be broken** - *The Scripture cannot be broken (John 10:35 KJV).*
- **The Word of God is eternal** - *For ever, O LORD, thy word is settled in heaven... every one of thy righteous judgments endureth for ever (Psalm 119:89 & 160 KJV).*
- **The Bible is true** - *Thy word is true from the beginning (Psalm 119:160 KJV).*

- **The Word of God protects you and the USA** - *His truth shall be thy shield and buckler (Psalm 91:4 KJV).*
- **Scripture defeats the devil** - *Young men, because ye are strong, and the word of God abideth in you, and ye have overcome the wicked one (1 John 2:14 KJV).*
- **The Bible is living and powerful** - *For the word of God is living and powerful, and sharper than any two-edged sword, piercing even to the division of soul and spirit, and of joints and marrow, and is a discerner of the thoughts and intents of the heart (Hebrews 4:12 KJV).*
- **The Holy Bible is pure** - *The words of the LORD are pure words: as silver tried in a furnace of earth, purified seven times (Psalm 12:6 KJV).*
- **The Word of God will outlast the earth** - *For verily I say unto you, Till heaven and earth pass, one jot or one tittle shall in no wise pass from the law, till all be fulfilled (Matthew 5:18 KJV).*
- **God's Word makes you and America prosperous** - *This book of the law shall not depart out of thy mouth; but thou shalt meditate therein day and night, that thou mayest observe to do according to all that is written therein: for then thou shalt make thy way prosperous, and then thou shalt have good success (Joshua 1:8 KJV).*

Jesus Christ accepted the authority of the Word of God and He quoted Scripture to defeat Satan. We also resist the devil by using the Bible. The devil knows that Scripture is the absolute authority, so when we speak and do God's Word the devil is defeated every time (Matthew 4:3-11). By the name of Jesus, the Word of God, and Jesus' blood, God gives Christians power over the devil.

Scripture is without error; every word is true. Every coma (i.e., jot) and dot (i.e., tittle) is true.

Live Daily with the LORD as Your Lawgiver

To do God's will, our founders established that our laws are from Scripture. With wisdom they made Christian laws and expect us to keep them, including to honor God by traditional marriage. This is because the Bible is the bedrock of the USA's legal system.

The Supreme Court affirmed, *It is well known that for our present form of government we are greatly indebted to his [Justice James Wilson's] exertions and influence... he states that profaneness and blasphemy [of God] are offences punishable by fine and imprisonment, and that Christianity is part of the common law.*[1] Wilson signed both the Declaration of Independence and the Constitution; George Washington appointed him to the original Supreme Court.

Human law must rest its authority, ultimately, upon the authority of that law, which is divine,[2] taught Justice Wilson, as the first law professor at the University of Pennsylvania.

By acknowledging God is our lawgiver, you bring justice to the USA and remove corruption. So praying a prayer like this makes a difference, "Father, You reign. I only recognize Your laws. I thank You that You are filling the USA with Your laws right now. In Jesus' name. Amen." Then publicly stand up and say, "The LORD is our lawgiver; He only blesses laws that are based on the Bible."

To Fear God Is the True Meaning of Presidential

Since God is a covenant God, He commands us to have our government in covenant with Him (Isaiah 9:6 & 33:22). This means to choose leaders who are in covenant. Perhaps, the primary metric of the maturity of the USA in Christ is how strong is our *covenant Christian nation government*. This is a government that follows the *7 Bible Truths*.

Why haven't we had a strong Christian government like our founders? The reasons are:

1. Pastors stopped teaching to vote for Christians only.
2. People voted for ungodly candidates.

A Christian government means protection of God-given rights. Other amazing benefits are we have Christians honored, Christian laws, better jobs, a wiser nation, and God's protection—like the America we love. A secret our founders knew is that elections are about voting to please God.

For pastors to teach on politics is more than to say to vote for *family values,* which has included voting for unbelievers. It is to choose Christians who make laws based on the Bible. Corruption results when pulpits are silent on politics. If pastors don't teach how to vote, people turn to the world.

The media also tries to tell us if a candidate is presidential or not and if they know foreign policy or not. But according to what definition? God's definition of presidential is to *fear God*. The best foreign policy is to have God's protection and favor. He does care about leaders and gives these instructions:

- *Thou shalt provide out of all the people able men, such as fear God, men of truth, hating covetousness; and place such over them, to be rulers of thousands, and rulers of hundreds, rulers of fifties, and rulers of tens:* (Exodus 18:21 KJV).

- *Be ye not unequally yoked together with unbelievers: for what fellowship has righteousness with unrighteousness?... Therefore come out from among them... and I will receive you...* (2 Corinthians 6:14-18 KJV)
- *He that is chief, as he that doth serve* (Luke 22:26 KJV).
- *In the image of God created he him* (Genesis 1:27 KJV).
- *Proclaim liberty throughout all the land unto all the inhabitants thereof* (Leviticus 25:10 KJV).

We have hope of our land healing by each of us pledging to choose Christian representatives from school boards to president. Our Lawmaker says to choose leaders based on five qualities and our forefathers fulfilled these requirements.

The Bible's Five Requirements for Leaders

America is great because of choosing Christian leaders. Here are God's requirements for leaders:

1. Able Christians Who Fear God *Exodus 18:21, 2 Cor. 6:14-18*

- They know the LORD is our Lawgiver, Judge, and King, so they follow the Holy Bible (Isaiah 33:22).
- Their goal is the true American Dream of advancing the Kingdom of our Lord Jesus Christ.
- Obeying God, they are pro-life and for traditional marriage only, and call for schools to daily read the Bible and have Christian prayer (Matthew 5:21, 2 Peter 2:6, Isaiah 59:21).
- As Jesus Christ serves the church, they serve Americans (Luke 22:26).

- They believe that our national security is first *In God We Trust* (Mark 12:31, Psalm 121:1 & 146:3-5).
- They have a Biblical view of the USA's war policy, which is defensive (just cause) non-aggressive wars. If in war, they call to quickly win the war.

2. Call for Christian Religious Liberty *Mark 12:30, Gal. 5:1*

- Following God, they boldly stand up to have Christian religious liberty throughout the USA (Matthew 4:10).
- They understand that the Constitution was written by Christians to protect Christians to serve the LORD.

3. Insist to Have God-given Rights *Genesis 1:27, Acts 5:29*

- Since our rights are endowed by our Creator and can never be surrendered, they affirm our Biblical rights.
- They are known for defending our unalienable rights of life, liberty, the pursuit of happiness, property, and conscience.

4. Truthful *Exodus 18:21*

- They are known for honesty not lying.
- They condemn all unconstitutional acts, so they don't limit our rights, but they limit government's power.

5. Hate Covetousness *Exodus 8:21*

- They refuse to take what belongs to *We the People*.
- With verifiable histories, they prove that they are effective at eliminating unjust taxes and cutting debts.
- As the Bible teaches, they promote self-government.

More benefits of a Christian government are:

- God commands it
- To welcome Jesus Christ
- We keep covenant with God

- To have the Kingdom of God
- God blesses us rather than judges us
- Voting for non-Christians causes Christian persecution
- Evil men cause the country to go the wrong direction
- Without Christian leaders we have unholy laws

Some say voting is choosing a president or mayor, not a pastor. But God says, *the LORD has sought him a man after his own heart* (1 Samuel 13:14 KJV). Moses, Joshua, David, Asa, and Josiah are among God's greatest political leaders. They all taught to obey God's Word, as did our founders.

Others vote on how someone looks on the outside, but God says, *Look not on his countenance, or on the height of his stature; because I have refused him: for the LORD seeth not as man seeth; for man looketh on the outward appearance, but the LORD looketh on the heart* (1 Samuel 16:7 KJV).

Isn't voting for non-Christians rejecting Jesus, because unbelievers are not in the body of Christ? The heathen are the children of the devil, so voting for them is choosing Satan to rule over oneself instead of God (John 8:44, 1 John 3:10).

Voting for non-Christians is also to turn away from the Kingdom of God, since God's enemies are of the power of darkness, not Jesus' Kingdom (Colossians 1:13). That is why there is a lower quality of life with worldly globalism. Our consciences should convict us to choose Christian leaders.

We know that most of the problems the USA faces are from choosing non-Christian leaders. *Shouldest thou help the ungodly, and love them that hate the LORD? therefore is wrath upon thee from before the LORD* (2 Chronicles 19:2 KJV).

John Jay co-authored the Federalist Papers and he believed this verse applied to voting.[3] Jay who started the Supreme Court said it is our duty to "select and prefer Christians" for leaders. He became a ministry president and worked for God's Word to abound throughout our nation.

God says, *whosoever therefore will be a friend of the world is the enemy of God* (James 4:4 KJV). *Love not the world, neither the things that are in the world. If any man love the world, the love of the Father is not in him* (1 John 2:15 KJV).

If we vote for someone who doesn't fear God, then not only are we voting for God's enemies, but these verses show that we become God's enemy too. Overlooking this part of God's Word caused the USA's safety to be at stake. However, by voting for those in Christ we are God's friend and blessed.

Political Judgments

There are consequences for choosing people who don't fear God as leaders. Israel was destroyed by Egypt when they turned to Egypt for help instead of God. The troubles are:

1. God's wrath *2 Chronicles 19:2*
2. Being cursed - *Blessed is the man that walketh not in the counsel of the ungodly, nor standeth in the way of sinners, nor sitteth in the seat of the scornful... Therefore the ungodly shall not stand in the judgment, nor sinners in the congregation of the righteous. For the LORD knoweth the way of the righteous: but the way of the ungodly shall perish. Psalm 1:1 and 5-6 KJV*
3. God uses the wicked in judgment *Ezekiel 23, Romans 1:28*
4. Turning away from sonship with God - *Come out from among them, and be ye separate... touch not the*

77

unclean thing; and I will receive you. And will be a
Father unto you, and ye shall be my sons and
daughters. 2 Corinthians 6:17-18 KJV

The good news is voting for Christians gives blessings, including ending the persecution of Christians. Some say vote for *family values,* but that is not enough, since it supports those who believe in families but aren't required to be faithful Christians. Instead, the Biblical way is to only support Christian leaders who diligently follow God. As a result, families are protected with Christian leaders.

Churches staying out of politics put our nation, cities, and lives in danger. We must make the commitment to only choose Christian leaders. Some say it is our civic duty to vote, even if we vote for the lesser of two evils. However, when is it right to disobey God? He commands us to vote for Christians. If a Christian isn't running, then every church should have ongoing prayer and fasting for God to give us Christian leaders and so we don't provoke God by helping the ungodly.

The Bible Is the Rock
on Which Our Republic Rests

God's Word makes the USA safe. The biggest threat to our national security is the people not following the Bible.

Jesus said, *Whosoever... heareth my sayings, and doeth them, I will shew you to whom he is like: He is like a man which built an house, and digged deep, and laid the foundation on a rock: and when the flood arose, the stream beat vehemently upon that house, and could not shake it: for it was founded upon a rock. But he that heareth, and doeth not, is like a man that without a foundation built an house upon the earth; against which the stream did beat vehemently, and immediately it fell; and the ruin... was great.* (Luke 6:47-49 KJV)

Christian Laws Heal Our Land

In this modern world some may think that we can't have Biblical laws now. But we need to think this over. Would we really lose our freedom by following God? Eve only knew her relationship with God and Adam. She was deceived by a lie and then had to face judgment and lose many blessings.

At which point was she truly free? When she walked and talked with God? Or when she exercised her free will to do things her way? We don't realize it, but we are losing our freedom and civil liberties because of judgment for dishonoring God with disobedience. So we need to ask ourselves if we are free following our will, or choosing to follow God's will?

Unreasonable people give excuses to resist God and not to honor His Holy Word like, "respect all beliefs," "tolerance," "coexist," or "diversity," but we know that the Bible says, *God is angry with the wicked every day* (Psalm 7:11 KJV). We see that Christian bakers, photographers, and others are losing jobs and being bullied because of "diversity". The word "diversity" has often been a code word for sin and anti-American ways that degrade the USA and bring judgment.

Ever since the garden of Eden, Satan has been attacking God's Word. So it is the devil who tries to lead people astray not to build the USA on the Rock of God's Word.

To have God bless us, we must follow what Scripture teaches. We can't add to what God says and we can't subtract from it either. We are protected by following His Word!

The good news is that God's Word filling our nation defeats Satan and evil. That is why I ask you to join me in praying often, *Father, we submit the USA to You in entirety. We want Your Word to fill our nation. In Jesus' name. Amen.*

To ensure that the USA was known for Christian character, our founders worked for all to know God's Word. This is one reason our government printed the Holy Bible and put it in schools so children would have piety and virtue.

Every law against the Bible is unjust. If we let our representatives defy God, then He judges us for this covenant breaking act. We know the First Amendment forbids Congress from making a law prohibiting the free exercise of Christianity. This means that laws against Christians are illegal according to the Constitution.

Who will be bold enough to put the Ten Commandments back in courts? All of them have been in our laws. Why would God bless us for pagan laws? Abraham Lincoln said, *without [the Bible] we could not know right from wrong.*[4] To love God is to love His Word. To show our love for God, we can often pray, *Father, You are my and the USA's lawgiver. I and the USA follow Your Word. In Jesus' name. Amen.*

Prosperity Comes By Obeying God's Word

Doing God's will, which is to do what the Bible teaches, causes blessings to come to you and the USA and makes our way prosperous. Jesus said, *seek ye first the kingdom of God, and his righteousness; and all these things shall be added unto you.* (Matthew 6:33 KJV). Look at these verses and see why and how God promises to prosper us:

- "... if thou shalt hearken diligently unto the voice of the LORD thy God, to observe and to do all his commandments... the LORD thy God will set thee on high above all nations of the earth: And all these blessings shall come on thee, and overtake thee..." (Deuteronomy 28:1-2 KJV)

- "This book of the law shall not depart out of thy mouth; but thou shalt meditate therein day and night, that thou mayest observe to do according to all that is written therein: for then thou shalt make thy way prosperous, and then thou shalt have good success." (Joshua 1:8 KJV)

We are always to love God, not money—even after God blesses us financially and with wealth. *For the love of money is the root of all evil* (1 Timothy 6:10 KJV). No one wants to forget God. So, let's make sure we put Him first in every part of our lives every day. An easy check that confirms God is our priority is to see if we are following all *7 Bible Truths.*

Americans Love the Holy Bible

There is a saying that I love. It is the USA is the land of the Bible. But we must work to continue as the land of God's Word and fill all fifty states with verses like, *Blessed is the nation whose God is the LORD* (Psalm 33:12 KJV) and *the LORD is our lawgiver* (Isaiah 33:22 KJV).

The Bible is the book the Jamestown Settlers, Pilgrims, and Puritans brought with them. The Bible is the book that founded America and it is the book that saves the USA! Our duty is to teach all our nation that the inspiration, sufficiency, and supremacy of God's Word is what sets it far above every other book. The Bible is the infallible Word of God and our final authority for all matters of faith and practice.

We know that God's written Word is the only reliable rule of faith. There is nothing truthful that opposes the Bible. God's Word is the only standard that Americans have for doctrine and laws. Everything contradicting Scripture is a lie.

Only the Bible heals our souls. There is no self-help book, seminar, or anything that will benefit our well being like His Word. The Bible puts our lives back together and leads us to Heaven. God speaks to us when we read His Word and the Bible is the only book that God requires us to read.

Next, we will learn how the USA's true ruler gives us protection and liberty.

✝ Prayer

Father, Americans love Your Word. You are the USA's Lawgiver. We ask for the Holy Bible to fill our homes, government, schools, courts, and military. We agree that Christianity is part of the common law. In Jesus' name. Amen.

✓ Reflection Questions

1. *What is Jesus Christ telling us in Luke 6:46-49?*
2. *Why does God protect us for having the Bible as the Rock on which our Republic rests? Give examples.*
3. *Is the LORD your lawgiver? Explain.*

6

Fourth Truth—Jesus Rules the USA

"The LORD is our King..."
Isaiah 33:22 KJV

Tensions were high. Resistance to tyrants was publicly viewed as obedience to God and liberty for every American. England saw that the people of our nation were confident that Jesus wanted them to obey Him, not King George. The English appointed governor of Boston reported in 1774, *If you ask an American, who is his master? He will tell you he has none, nor any governor but Jesus Christ.*[1]

Patriotically, our founders sounded, *No king but King Jesus,* as an American Revolution motto. This famous battle cry affirms that Jesus Christ rules our nation and the USA lives for Him. This is why we are *One Nation Under God!*

They recognized Jesus' authority and we need to follow their example and confess that Jesus is our King and authority.

Obeying Jesus Makes America Great

Every person has a king. Who is your king? The person that you obey is your ruler. There are two choices:

- Jesus Christ – the King of the Kingdom of God, or
- The devil – the king of the power of darkness.

Everyone serves one of these two kings, Jesus Christ or Satan. However, choosing the right king makes the difference between living in:

- Light, truth, protection, and liberty with King Jesus, or
- Darkness, lies, danger, and tyranny with the devil.

This is important because each of us will give an account of our lives to Jesus Christ on the Judgment Day, so we must follow Him (2 Corinthians 5:10). We are stewards of what God has given us and want to hear Christ say, "Well done," to our work (Matthew 25:21 KJV).

You must make the decision that Jesus is your King, since after Adam's fall people are naturally born under the sinful nature. The people not following Jesus Christ are under Satan's power, even if they serve themselves or a person in sin (Colossians 1:13).

Who we follow is an urgent matter that affects the safety of our daily lives and the future of the USA. We see our country's survival is at stake with many troubles—from politicians opposing our God-given rights to terrorism.

Fourth Bible Truth	Have no king but King Jesus
for protection and blessings *Isaiah 33:22, Phil. 2:11*	*Why? Jesus brings the Kingdom of God's blessings, including safety and liberty.*

The Fourth Bible Truth is God protects you, gives you liberty, justice, and righteousness, and saves the USA for having "no king but King Jesus". America is great because of having Jesus as our King. Disobeying Jesus means there is danger, tyranny, injustice, and sin. But with King Jesus we are free from communism, golbalists, and the New World Order.

In power and majesty Jesus reigns, whether we submit to Him or not. Psalm 47:7-9 says, *For God is the King of all the earth: sing ye praises with understanding. God reigneth over the heathen: God sitteth upon the throne of his holiness... the shields of the earth belong unto God: he is greatly exalted.*

If you are a Christian, then you know Jesus Christ as your Saviour. He gave Himself to save you, all He has including His life. Imagine the day and what you will do when He wraps His hands with the nail prints around you and says, "I love you" and welcomes you to Heaven. Jesus Christ is the only one who can save your soul. If you are not a Christian, today is the day to call on Him to save you from your sins. The moment you are born again, God delivers you from the devil's kingdom, the power of darkness, and translates you into the Kingdom of His dear Son. Jesus is your King (Col. 1:13).

Jesus is also the Son of Man who we identify with and He understands us. He lived a sinless life even though He was tempted in all things. As the Son of God, we worship Jesus Christ; He is God in the flesh. When we realize how majestic

85

He is and how much He cares for us by being crucified for us at Calvary, then we passionately declare I want to know Him more. His love for us increases our desire to be near Him.

Highly educated Paul, the apostle, counted all he gained as loss compared to knowing Jesus. *That I may know Him*, said Paul, as he daily yearned to walk close with the Lord (Philippians 3:10 KJV). The reward of knowing Jesus more is infinitely greater than other things in life. We know Him by reading the Bible, the Spirit, and spending time with Him.

Jesus Christ Is the Sovereign of the Universe

Jesus is unlike any other ruler because His Kingdom is grace and truth. He is the King of holiness. He wants you to be with Him because you have eternal life in Him. No other leader compares to our Lord who gave everything for you. The Kingdom of God is where liberty, abundance and peace exist, as well as righteousness, protection, joy, healing, and every good thing. Since Jesus is King of the Kingdom of God, serving Him is mandatory to solve our nation's problems.

Can you think of a good reason not to have Jesus as the USA's King? Why would God bless our nation and deliver us from politicians not listening to us if His Son is not our ruler?

From Adam to Samuel, God's people had no earthly king for they lived with God as their King directly. With the LORD as King, Noah was spared judgment, Israel defeated the greatest military power, and Joshua took Jericho. Our founders covenanted and made Jesus King of the USA and our republic has seen grace, miracles, and victories from God.

Since Jesus is the ruler of everything, we are to live exalting Him above every other person. God testifies, *That at the name of Jesus every knee should bow, of things in heaven, and things in earth, and things under the earth; And that every tongue should confess that Jesus Christ is Lord, to the glory of God the Father* (Philippians 2:10-11 KJV).

We honor Him as superior to all political leaders for He is the *KING OF KINGS, AND LORD OF LORDS* (Revelation 19:16; 1:5, 1 Timothy 6:15 KJV). He is subject to no one, but the Father, and all things are subject to Him. All things are done according to His counsel and all authority in heaven and earth has been given to Him (Colossians 1:16, Matthew 28:18).

Jesus sits at the right hand of God the Father. Higher than the angels, His throne is forever and ever; of His Kingdom there shall be no end (Hebrews 1:8, Luke 1:33). We know that His wrath is on the earthly leaders who don't follow Him (Psalm 2:2-5). Pharaoh found out the LORD is a man of war.

Jesus was in the beginning with God; He is our Creator. All things were made by Him with the Father and Holy Spirit (John 1:1-3). We exalt Him because He is God and in Him all things exist (Hebrews 1:2-3, 6, Colossians 1:17). The earth and the heavens will perish, but He will always exist (2 Peter 3:10-11). He is the Alpha and the Omega, the Beginning and the End, the First and the Last (Revelation 22:13).

As the Judge of mankind, we have confidence that He will not acquit the wicked. He knows everything about everyone and He knows more about each person than even they know of themselves. He pardons the sins of all who come to Him.

Along with the Father and the Holy Spirit, Jesus Christ is Elohim (our Creator), Jehovah (my LORD God), Adonai (master and Lord), El Shaddai (God Almighty, my supply, my nourishment), Jehovah Jireh (my provider), Jehovah Rapha (my healer), Jehovah Nissi (my banner, victory), Jehovah Mikadesh (my sanctifier), Jehovah Tsidkenu (my righteousness), Jehovah Shalom (my peace), Jehovah Rohi (my shepherd), and Jehovah Shammah (the LORD is there). Jesus Christ is the great I AM.

Having no king but King Jesus isn't reserved only for when we get to Heaven. It is a daily, moment-by-moment walk with Him that gives you God's favor instead of alienation. Think how much favor God gives you when you say Jesus is your King. To live with Jesus as your leader, first acknowledge Him as your King. Then during the day thank Him for His goodness and obey Him by faith, submitting to His authority (Matthew 16:24).

Why do we say, "Jesus Christ is Lord of the USA"? The answer is the USA has the Kingdom of God blessings through Him. We have liberty, prosperity, peace, brotherly love, and every good thing. To be free of dictators, Shariah law, and corruption, then daily live with Jesus Christ as the leader of our nation. Where He rules, there are no evil rulers. That is why tyrants oppose Christianity, but Jesus is stronger than all evil persons. He removes corruption to protect His people.

Our thoughts are to be on Jesus Christ because He is glorious. When I think about His dominion, kindness, love, majesty, and power, I worship Him! I declare, "Jesus, You are my King. I want to know You more; I surrender everything to You." Heaven proclaims, *Worthy is the Lamb that was slain to receive power, and riches, and wisdom, and strength, and honour, and glory, and blessing* (Revelation 5:12 KJV)! What is your response to Jesus?

Is Jesus Your King?

Let's look at four common levels of having Jesus as our King. The following shows where people are at:

1. **Rebellion** – This person serves self or man not King Jesus.
2. **Mental assent that Jesus is King** – Many Christians are at this level where they agree that Jesus is their King but don't pray and think when making decision, "What does Jesus want me to do?"
3. **Partial surrender to the KING OF KINGS** – At this level, a person is willing to obey God, but only occasionally takes a public stand for Jesus Christ.
4. **Total surrender to King Jesus** – This is the level God desires. We see the disciples left all and followed Jesus. Also, the founding fathers obeyed Jesus and proclaimed: "no king but King Jesus" instead of man. At this level, Jesus defeats your enemies continuously.

Our founders taught it is our duty to do God's will. So if Jesus is your leader, "obey God, rather than men" (Acts 5:29).

Americans have "No King but King Jesus"

Americans believe it is our country's duty to serve God and that human authority is under God's authority. That is one reason why real Americans have Jesus as their leader. Famous American pastors, like Jonas Clark, taught, "God is governor among the nations," from Psalm 22:28 (KJV).

President George Washington reminds us to, "unite in most humbly offering our prayers and supplications to the great Lord and Ruler of Nations..."[2] Jesus gives us much to be thankful for. Unbelievers miss so much by not having God's Kingdom. No forgiveness. No protection. No deliverance. However, with Jesus ruling us, we have all these blessings.

The good news is it is easy for our nation to have abundant blessings again. The key is to realize all blessings come through Jesus Christ.

Romans 13: Is Jesus or Sinful Government King?

To save the USA, we have an important decision to make of who we serve, so we stop provoking God. Some think they are to "submit to government no matter what" and try to justify it using Romans 13. But is that the message of the Bible? Instead of blessings, the sins of politicians disobeying Jesus Christ cause God's wrath to our nation.

God removed Israel and Judah for the people tolerating the sins of the evil kings. The fruit of submitting to bad government against God is captivity. Like Israel, people may be killed and be slaves for following a president, congress or supreme court against God (1 Kings 13:34, 2 Kings 21:11-13). But liberty is the fruit of obeying God rather than sinful leaders. This is proven with God freeing our founders and Moses for following God instead of tyrants (2 Cor. 3:17).

Americans are for good government that serves God and we reject corrupt politicians, because that is how God is. He is sovereign. He is with those who are with Him (2 Chronicles 15:2, 2 Timothy 2:12). He says to leaders, *Kiss the Son, lest He be angry* and *they perish from the way, when His wrath is kindled* (Psalm 2:12 KJV). The USA submits to Jesus Christ because the government is upon His shoulder (Isaiah 9:6).

We believe the Declaration of Independence is a rejection of ungodly rule. King George no longer rewarded good and punished evil as God commands (Romans 13:4, 1 Peter 2:14). So our founders fulfilled the responsibility of New Testament believers *to obey God rather than men* (Acts 5:29 KJV). This is the rule of Scripture. To love God is the First Commandment, so God is our ruler not anyone else. To love our neighbor as ourselves is the Second Commandment. But tyrants imposing their will on people, break these laws. That cannot be right.

HOLY BIBLE Bible Principle

With Jesus as your King, you see the Kingdom of God.

The Hebrew midwives, Rahab, Daniel, Joseph and Mary, the wise men, Peter, Paul, John, and all the righteous followed God not sinful rulers. God says, *The midwives feared God, and did not as the king of Egypt commanded them... Therefore God dealt well with the midwives (Exodus 1:17, 20 KJV).* Since the Bible teaches that God blesses those who obey Him by refusing to follow unjust laws against Scripture, it is an erroneous belief to "submit to government no matter what".

Hope: Good Government Honors Christians

The misinterpretation of Romans 13 has caused trouble; it does not bring God's favor. Even with evil laws that bring God's wrath, some say, "obey them". But it is a sin to support oppression, or to reward evil and punish good.

American history gives us the correct teaching. Among those who found Christian refuge in America are the Huguenots, where many of our courageous founders come from. They put God first. A Huguenot tract, "A Defense of Liberty against Tyrants," answers this question: Are we to have obedience to princes or God? All are to do God's will for *all men... are His servants, farmers, officers and vassals, and owe account and acknowledgement to Him, according to that which He has committed to their dispensation; the higher their place is, the greater their account must be.*[3]

Liberty sermons like "A Discourse Concerning Unlimited Submission and Non-resistance to the Higher Powers" in 1750 by Jonathan Mayhew say it is good to submit to leaders serving God, but wrong to obey *tyrannical, oppressive rulers* as Romans 13 means leaders *are supposed to fulfill the pleasure of God... But how is this an argument for obedience to such rulers as do not perform the pleasure of God, by doing good; but the pleasure of the devil, by doing evil; and such as are not, therefore, God's ministers, but the devil's!*[4]

Under God *We the People* are in charge. Elected officials are not above the Bible, us, or the Constitution (1 Peter 2:13). Reading Romans 13 in the King James Bible explains it better for it uses "higher powers" not "governing authorities". God is the highest power. Then the Constitution is the "supreme" law of the land. Looking at it this way matches the rest of the Bible.

Moses obeyed God as his King not Pharaoh. *By faith he forsook Egypt, not fearing the wrath of the king; for he endured, as seeing Him who is invisible* (Hebrews 11:27 KJV).

A mother is often the strongest earthly bond, but King Asa knew honoring God over his mother was God's will and would heal the land. So Asa *removed her from being queen, because she had made an idol in a grove: and Asa cut down her idol, and stamped it, and burnt it* (2 Chronicles 15:16 KJV).

Some say, "honor the king," but the USA isn't a man-made monarchy (1 Peter 2:17). Remember, we are a Christian Republic with a Constitution, so churches must correctly teach to: (1) Honor the Bible above all and (2) Honor the Constitution. Those who say to submit to congress, the president, or the courts when they violate the Constitution dishonor God's Word and break the law. Take time and confess this sin to God to heal out land if you have done this.

As a note, 1 Peter 2:17 says, *Honour all men. Love the brotherhood. Fear God. Honour the king.* The word "honour" is used for all men and the king. We need more people saying to fear God. Jesus said, *fear not them which kill the body, but are not able to kill the soul: but rather fear Him which is able to destroy both soul and body in hell* (Matthew 10:28 KJV).

We honor politicians, courts, and police who serve God and follow the Constitution. But how can we honor those who violate the First Amendment and persecute Christians, or against our safety disregard the Second Amendment and try to disarm Americans, or violate the Fourth Amendment with warrantless searches, as these acts are against Americans?

The church's greatest civic duty is to endorse Christian political candidates. Churches have never been taxed to begin with, as the First Amendment forbids taxing churches. But politicians, by the Johnson Amendment in 1954, talked many churches to be non-profit 501(c)(3)'s with the catch they wouldn't endorse a candidate to keep their tax free status. Ministers fell for the scheme to not follow the Constitution, the law of the land after God's Word. As a result of pastors being silent, Christians have been persecuted, corruption abounds, and the USA's survival is at risk. To save our nation, churches either must speak up politically as a non-profit or start a NOT non-profit ministry and speak up politically.

Donald Trump and Mike Pence want congress to get rid of the corrupt Johnson Amendment. This is a sign of God's favor from those who follow the powerful *7 Bible Truths*. We saw God speak through President Trump when he said he was going to "destroy" the Johnson Amendment. This is a priority to make the USA great, because it shows that Jesus is King of the USA, not tyranny. Every pastor and Christian should boldly speak up for God, even with the corrupt Johnson Amendment, which the Holy Bible and the First Amendment say is illegal.

To glorify God and so Americans have freedom, the Gospel of Jesus Christ must never be compromised. You may have realized that Churches that won't speak up politically can't save the USA. All glory to God; because I teach the Gospel I am seeing revival nationwide. The USA is a covenant Christian nation and it is our duty to keep and protect our nation that belongs to God for God's glory.

King Jesus Saves the USA

Be encouraged for God promises, *The LORD is our king; He will save us* (Isaiah 33:22 KJV). We have great hope because God rewards faith by answering prayer. We see time after time in the Bible that the righteous *through faith subdued kingdoms* (Hebrews 11:33 KJV). With faith in God, America's enemies are defeated. Jesus Christ is the USA's Deliverer.

Our founders needed deliverance from tyrants, so our "first national anthem" in 1770 says, *We fear them not, we trust in God. New England's God forever reigns.* This song, *Chester,* was boldly sung in churches, as soldiers marched, and in homes to show that Americans are for liberty and resist tyranny. It was written by famous hymnist William Billings.

Singing about our King and trusting in Him gives our nation deliverance. "My Country 'Tis of Thee" turns our hearts to exalt God. *Our fathers' God, to Thee, author of liberty... Protect us by Thy might, Great God, our King.*

Rejoice! Having *no king but King Jesus* always defeats America's enemies. Serving Him is why we stand up for life, liberty, and the pursuit of happiness. Everyone must understand that it is Jesus who makes the USA free! As true Americans we love Him! With Jesus as our leader we show God that He has our allegiance and He ends our judgment.

Our liberty-loving nation must have *no king but King Jesus* so we are on God's side and have His freedom. Will you affirm that Jesus is the USA's King? If so, then with love for God in your heart, share with as many people as you can, *The LORD is our king; He will save us* (Isaiah 33:22 KJV).

Next, we discover an easy tool to share the good news and raise up the next generations as godly Americans.

✝ Prayer

Father, Jesus Christ is my King and the King of the USA.
The USA obeys Him, not anyone else. We thank You that right
now He is removing everything against Him from the USA.
In Jesus' name. Amen.

✓ Reflection Questions

1. *How do you live with no king but King Jesus? Explain.*
2. *Why do those refusing to say Jesus is King of the USA cause God's judgment on our nation?*
3. *Why did God greatly bless our founders and Moses for obeying Him rather than ungodly rule?*
4. *With more people calling on Jesus as King of the USA, what additional blessings would you have?*

7

Fifth Truth—Disciple Hearts to Be Like Jesus

"Teaching them to observe all things whatsoever I have commanded you..." Jesus
Matthew 28:20 KJV

God desires for our nation to have hearts like Jesus, so we glorify God and do good to man. Living like Jesus makes our citizens exceptional. Our forefathers faithfully advanced the Kingdom of God to help America grow in Christ, with piety and virtue. As stewards, they discipled the USA as their priority. Now it is our turn to teach to observe all things Jesus commanded us. We will have great wisdom and injustice will end (Matthew 28:19-20).

Jesus gave us the Great Commission and He said that part of our vital work for Him is *that repentance and remission of sins should be preached in His name among all nations* (Luke 24:47 KJV). The *all nations* includes our beloved USA.

The Fifth Bible Truth is God will protect you and prosper the USA by making disciples of the country. Keeping covenant to raise godly generations creates a safe nation with upright and law-abiding citizens instead of a country with crime and riots. Making Christian disciples of our nation makes the USA exceptional. But it is ignoble to have children who do not know God's Word and live in sin.

Fifth Bible Truth for protection and blessings Matt. 28:19-20, Is. 59:21	Make disciples of the USA Why? To raise godly generations.

We should often ask ourselves, "What can we do for God and country?" We can teach that the LORD is the God of our nation and help put Bible reading back in every school. Let's make disciples. This is the next step to make the USA great.

12 American Ways to Make Disciples

To have hearts like Jesus, teach the following:

1. **Serve the LORD only**—not strange gods or anything else. *Matthew 4:10, Exodus 20:3*
2. **Have no king but King Jesus:** God is sovereign; we obey God's government. *Isaiah 9:6 & 33:22, Philippians 2:11, Revelation 19:6, 2 Timothy 2:12*
3. **Demand Christian religious liberty:** We advance the Kingdom of our Lord Jesus. *Mark 12:30, Gal. 5:1*
4. **Man is created with dignity:** Americans demand our God-given unalienable rights—*including life, liberty, the pursuit of happiness, property, and conscience. Genesis 1:27, Acts 5:29, Declaration of Independence*

5. **The USA has traditional marriage only**—One man and one woman; we believe in sexual purity with no adultery or fornication. *Jude 7, 1 Corinthians 6:9-11*

6. **Instruct children to know God:** Daily read the Holy Bible and have Christian prayer in schools. *Isaiah 59:21*

7. **The LORD is our Lawgiver:** God only blesses Christian laws based on the Bible. *Luke 6:47-49, Is. 33:22*

8. **Work to have a covenant Christian nation Government** immediately that:

    1) Are Christians who fear God Ex. 18:21, 2 Cor. 6:14-18

    2) Calls for Christian religious liberty Mark 12:30, Gal. 5:1

    3) Insists we have God-given rights Gen 1:27, Acts 5:29

    4) Is truthful Exodus 18:21

    5) Hates covetousness Exodus 18:21

9. **Support Christians** in politics, business, and organizations—not the heathen. *2 Chronicles 19:2*

10. **Our Christian nation is pro-life.** *Matthew 5:17*

11. **Serve God, not mammon (money).** *Matthew 6:24*

12. **Biblically pray for government.** Pray daily for the people of our nation and government to live the five points of #8 above. You can get a prayer brochure at www.USA.church.

12 Decisions to Have a Heart Like Jesus

If we want our hearts to be like Jesus, then we need to show we are on the LORD's side. With love in our hearts, we must disciple everyone we know to do the same by teaching the following. Will you make these decisions:

Decision 1: I serve the LORD only and renounce all other gods. The USA is a Christian nation.

- Jesus said, " Thou shalt worship the Lord thy God, and him only shalt thou serve" (Matthew 4:10 KJV).
- "Those nations only are blessed whose God is the Lord." Abraham Lincoln[1]
- "This is a Christian nation" Supreme Court[2]
- The blessings of serving the LORD mean that we are God's people with His blessings, abundance and protection (2 Corinthians 6:16, Psalm 33:12, Psalm 37:40); The judgments for false gods are perishing (Deuteronomy 32:16-18, 8:19-20).

Decision 2: The LORD is my King. The USA has no king but King Jesus. We obey God's government.

- "The government shall be upon His shoulder" (Isaiah 9:6 KJV).
- "For the LORD is our judge, the LORD is our lawgiver, the LORD is our king; He will save us" (Isaiah 33:22 KJV).
- "At the name of Jesus every knee should bow... every tongue should confess that Jesus Christ is Lord" (Phil. 2:10-11 KJV).
- Government, "Devoutly recognizing the Supreme Authority and just Government of Almighty God, in all the affairs of men and of nations..." Abraham Lincoln[1]
- The blessings of Jesus as our King are: God saves the USA, liberty, abundance, national security, and the Kingdom of God. The judgments for serving others are darkness, tyranny and destruction (Isaiah 33:22, Colossians 1:13, John 8:12, 2 Corinthians 3:17, Matthew 6:33, 1 Kings 13:34, Luke 18:6).

Decision 3: Like our founders, I call for Christian religious liberty, not religious liberty of false gods.

- "Stand fast therefore in the liberty wherewith Christ hath made us free" (Galatians 5:1 KJV).

- "Thou shalt love the Lord thy God with all thy heart, and with all thy soul, and with all thy mind, and with all thy strength" (Mark 12:30 KJV).
- Praying in Jesus' name and reading the Bible is Congress' first act. George Washington ordered the military to attend Christian church. The Bible was in schools from 1607-1962.
- The blessings for demanding Christian religious liberty are advancing the Kingdom of our Lord Jesus Christ and Christians are honored. The judgments for false gods are destruction (Matthew 28:19-20, Ezekiel 23).

Decision 4: I am created with dignity in the image of God. No one can take away my unalienable rights.

- "God created man in His own image" (Genesis 1:27 KJV).
- "We ought to obey God rather than men" (Acts 5:29 KJV).
- See the Declaration of Independence.
- The blessings for standing up for our God-given rights are Americans live free with our rights (2 Corinthians 3:17). The judgments for giving up rights is tyrants (Nehemiah 9:32-37).

Decision 5: God created male and female. To do His will, the USA has traditional marriage only (one man and one woman for a lifetime). The USA repents of fornication, adultery, and homosexual sin.

- "Now the body is not for fornication, but for the Lord; and the Lord for the body" (1 Corinthians 6:13 KJV).

"Be not deceived: neither fornicators... nor adulterers, nor effeminate, nor abusers of themselves with mankind... shall inherit the kingdom of God" (1 Corinthians 6:9-10 KJV).

- The blessings for God's Marriage of one man and one woman are strong families, God's favor, and more people go to Heaven. The judgments for dishonoring God are He destroys

homosexual nations and unrepentant sinners don't go to
Heaven (1 Corinthians 6:9-11, 2 Peter 2:6, Leviticus 18:25).

Decision 6: Children must know God. I will call for daily Bible reading and Christian prayer in schools.

- " As for me, this is my covenant with them, saith the LORD;
  My spirit that is upon thee, and my words which I have put
  in thy mouth, shall not depart out of thy mouth, nor out of
  the mouth of thy seed, nor out of the mouth of thy seed's
  seed, saith the LORD, from henceforth and for ever" (Isaiah
  59:21 KJV).
- "Education is useless without the Bible." Noah Webster[3]
- George Washington told Indians, "I am glad you have
  brought three of the children of your principal chiefs to be
  educated with us... You do well to wish to learn... above all,
  the religion of Jesus Christ. These will make you a greater
  and happier people than you are. Congress will do everything
  they can to assist you in this wise intention..."[4]
- The blessings for the Bible in schools are more children are
  saved and the USA has Christian character (Proverbs 22:6).
  The judgments for disobeying God are His wrath for
  breaking covenant and, sadly, more go to hell (Matthew
  16:26).

Decision 7: The LORD is our Lawgiver. God is righteous, so I want laws based on the Holy Bible.

- "The LORD is our lawgiver" (Isaiah 33:22 KJV).
- Whosoever... heareth my sayings, and doeth them, I will shew
  you to whom he is like: He is like a man which built an house,
  and digged deep, and laid the foundation on a rock: and
  when the flood arose, the stream beat vehemently upon that
  house, and could not shake it: for it was founded upon a rock.

But he that heareth, and doeth not, is like a man that without a foundation built an house upon the earth; against which the stream did beat vehemently, and immediately it fell; and the ruin... was great. (Luke 6:47-49 KJV)

- "Christianity is part of the common law" Supreme Court[5]
- "[The Holy Bible] is the Rock on which our Republic rests," Andrew Jackson.[6]
- The blessings for making Christian laws are national security, health, and blessings. The judgments for disobeying God with non-Christian laws are curses, the USA being destroyed, and sickness (Deuteronomy 28, Luke 6:47-48, Exodus 15:26).

Decision 8: I will work and pray to have a Christian government immediately, as this is God's will.

- "Be ye not unequally yoked together with unbelievers: for what fellowship has righteousness with unrighteousness? and what communion has light with darkness? ... or what part has he that believes with an infidel?" (2 Corinthians 6:14-15 KJV).
- "Provide out of all the people able men, such as fear God, men of truth, hating covetousness; and place such over them, to be rulers" (Exodus 18:21 KJV).
- "When the children of Israel cried unto the LORD, the LORD raised up a deliverer to the children of Israel, who delivered them" (Judges 3:9 KJV).
- The blessings for a Christian government are the USA is exalted and blessed in all things (Proverbs 14:34, Psalm 1:1). The judgments for a non-Christian government are God's wrath and shame as a nation (2 Chronicles 19:2, Prov. 14:34).

Decision 9: I support Christians in politics, business, and organizations, not the heathen.

- "Shouldest thou help the ungodly, and love them that hate the LORD? therefore is wrath upon thee from before the LORD" (2 Chronicles 19:2 KJV).
- The blessings of helping people, businesses, and ministries that follow God are He exalts our nation and rewards (Proverbs 14:34, Matthew 10:41). The judgments for helping the ungodly brings the wrath of the LORD and reproach (2 Chronicles 19:2, Proverbs 14:34).

Decision 10: God is pro-life so the USA is pro-life. I believe our country is to ban the sin of abortion again, honor father and mother, and repent of unjust wars.

- Jesus says, "Thou shalt not kill" (Matthew 5:21 KJV).
- "They sacrificed their sons and their daughters unto devils, and shed innocent blood... Thus were they defiled with their own works.. Therefore was the wrath of the LORD kindled against His people, so that He abhorred His own inheritance. And He gave them into the hand of the heathen; and they that hated them ruled over them. Their enemies also oppressed them... they were brought into subjection" (Psalm 106:37-42 KJV).
- "Honour thy father and mother" (Ephesians 6:2 KJV).
- "Love one another" (John 13:34 KJV).
- The blessings for being pro-life are a clear conscience, children, and happiness (Psalm 127:4-5). The judgments are God's wrath and tyrants as leaders, as is also the same judgment for unjust wars (Psalm 106:37-42). Honoring your father and mother results in long life (Deuteronomy 5:16).

Decision 11: I serve God, not mammon (money).

- "No man can serve two masters: for either he will hate the one, and love the other; or else he will hold to the one, and despise the other. Ye cannot serve God and mammon [riches]" (Matthew 6:24 KJV).
- The blessings for serving God are abundance (Matthew 6:33). The judgments for serving mammon (money) are God's wrath and many sorrows (1 Timothy 6:10).

Decision 12: I will pray Biblically for the people of our nation and our government to fear God.

Why do we pray for our leaders? The Bible says the reason is *that we may lead a quiet and peaceable life in all godliness and honesty* (1 Timothy 2:2 KJV). To get this result, God's will is that we pray for our representatives to fear God and to protect our God-given rights. This is more Biblical than praying for leaders to have wisdom since, *The fear of the LORD is the beginning of wisdom* (Proverbs 9:10 KJV). We must pray for all Americans to fear and love God, as under God *We the People* are in charge of our government.

While we do pray, "God bless America," we never pray for politicians dishonoring God's Word that God would strengthen, protect, and bless them. We know He forbids that and judgment comes to those who help God's enemies (2 Chronicles 19:2, Romans 1:32, Psalm 129:5-8).

If politicians refuse to serve God, the Bible teaches for us to cry out to God for Christians who fear God to immediately replace those disobeying God. This is so we don't suffer in judgment by perpetuating their sin (Judges 3:9, 2 Corinthians 6:14-18, 2 Samuel 23:3).

Daily Biblical Prayer for Government™

Father,

The USA serves Jesus Christ. We devoutly recognize Your "Supreme Authority and just Government... in all the affairs of men and of nations". We love You and we love one another. May we and our representatives, schools, courts, law enforcement, and military:

1) Fear You, 2) Call for Christian religious liberty,

3) Insist to have our God-given rights of life, liberty, the pursuit of happiness, property, conscience...,

4) Be truthful, and 5) Hate covetousness.

We cry out for Christian leaders to immediately replace those disobeying You.

One Nation Under God. In God We Trust.

In Jesus' name. Amen.

Pray this daily prayer at home and with your church; it is based on: Isaiah 9:6, Mark 12:30-31, Exodus 18:21, 2 Cor. 6:14-18, Luke 22:26, Genesis 1:27, Judges 3:9. Include "by Rev. Steven Andrew" to reuse.

Wednesdays: Nationwide Prayer and Fasting

In addition to these *12 Decisions to Have a Heart Like Jesus*, you and your church are invited to participate in: (1) Nationwide prayer and fasting; (2) Christians Uniting to Save the USA™; and (3) The American Disciple Making Team™.

To heal our land, we pray and fast for our nation to repent of everything against Jesus, since God only blesses us through His Son. Join every Wednesday and ask your church to pray:

Father,

We exalt You, LORD, as the God of the USA. May Your will be done. We seek You to heal our land. To glorify You, and as our founders believed, the USA: serves You only, insists to have Christian religious liberty, wants daily Bible reading and Christian prayer back in schools, is pro-life, and is for traditional marriage only. We desire to please You and we pray for everything against Jesus Christ to be removed from our nation in a peaceable way. We want a Christian government. As You say in Judges 3:9 and 2 Corinthians 6:14-18, we cry out for Christian leaders to immediately replace those disobeying You. Forgive our sins by Jesus' blood.

In Jesus' name. Amen.

2 Chronicles 7:14, Luke 11:2, Psalm 33:12, Matthew 4:10 & 5:21, Isaiah 59:21, 2 Peter 2:6, 1 John 3:8 & 1:7, Exodus 18:21, Judges 3:9, 2 Corinthians 6:14-18. Include "by Rev. Steven Andrew" to reuse.

Christians Uniting to Save the USA™

An amazing story is a conflict in the Continental Congress almost stopped our liberty from King George's oppression in 1774. Christians of different denominations weren't praying together due to denominational differences. So, to unite the USA in Christ and win the Revolutionary War, Samuel Adams arose and said, *I... can hear a prayer from a [Christian] gentleman of piety and virtue who was at the same time a friend to his country*[7] and the people agreed.

As Americans we must unite with every Christian of piety and virtue who loves the USA. If we have differences on doctrines, the seven things we must agree on are that we:

1. Insist to have Christian religious liberty and God-given rights.
2. Keep covenant the USA is a Christian nation—*The LORD is the God of the USA and we are His people.*
3. Call for Christian leaders in public service only, from school boards to president, not the heathen
4. Teach that *righteousness exalteth a nation: but sin is a reproach to any people.* Proverbs 14:34
5. Believe the Gospel of Jesus Christ.
6. Have the LORD as our Lawgiver with the Holy Bible as our final authority.
7. Obey the Constitution, which after the Holy Bible is the law of the land and protects our God-given rights.

See Chapters 2, 3 & 5 for the information for these items.

Be Part of the American Disciple Making Team™

God wants every heart of the USA to love Him. So, I ask you and your church to join the American Disciple Making Team™ (ADMT) at www.USA.church. God calls all fifty states to unite in Christ as His powerful American church.

Disciple making is to be part of our daily life. We make hearts to be like Jesus by sharing these 12 decisions and praying for our nation's hearts to love God more. Some ideas are to write articles or letters, make videos, blog, and start a home group to study this book. To make disciples, just share what you know of these Bible Truths.

How much time do you want to give to God? Can you give Him ten percent of your time? This is about two and half hours a day. This could be: (1) An hour in the morning seeking and worshipping God; (2) An hour disciple making (meeting with someone, or sharing Bible verses by mail or online, or crying out to God for mercy for our country, or praying for our nation's hearts to love and fear God); and, (3) A half hour devotional time with God before you go to bed.

If you aren't ready for two and half hours, could you give God an hour a day? That could be twenty minutes of prayer and Bible reading morning and evening, and twenty minutes of discipling. If you have a family, be sure they get part of your ministry time. This is the most important work. You can prayerfully schedule what you will do each day. For example:

Monday:	*5:00 - 6:00 pm*	*Disciple John*
Tuesday:	*5:00 - 6:00 pm*	*Share the 12 decisions online*
Wednesday:	*6:00 - 7:00 pm*	*Pray and fast for the USA*
Thursday:	*12:00 - 1:00 pm*	*Ask others to insist the USA has Christian religious liberty*

...

Daily:	*6:00 - 7:00 am*	*Pray and read Bible*
	9:30 - 10:00 pm	*Pray and read Bible*

I pray for every person and church in the American Disciple Making Team™ and give updates and tips, so let me know you joined at my website. Helping to make disciples with these important decisions gives you a larger ministry.

Next, we discover how to have victory over sin.

✝ Prayer

Father, the USA serves You. Help us make disciples
of our nation. In Jesus' name. Amen.

✓ Reflection Questions

1. *Why must the USA be discipled?*
2. *History affirms that raising godly generations makes America wealthy. Why is this?*
3. *In what ways can you help teach these 12 American ways to follow Jesus? What can your church do?*

8

Sixth Truth—Victory Over Sin

"He took courage,
and put away the abominable idols..."
2 Chronicles 15:8 KJV

History is filled with holy conflict when God's people rise up and publicly turn from their wicked ways and sinful relationships. With great courage King Asa and the people arose to stop the apathy about sin, so their troubles from God's judgment would end. As they used to do in Old Testament times before Jesus Christ came, the Bible shows that Judah killed the wicked people (2 Chronicles 15).

King Josiah also loved God and did the same (2 Kings 23:4-24). Likewise, in holy conflict Moses boldly called those on the LORD's side to kill the people refusing to repent, so God wouldn't destroy Israel when the people forsook Him by turning away from God to worship a molten calf (Exodus 32).

Today we remove evil differently; we *turn away* from those who refuse to repent (2 Timothy 3:5, Romans 16:7, 1

Corinthians 5:13, James 4:7). God wants us free of evil so we simply *separate* ourselves from those against God. We read the Old Testament accounts of killing through the New Testament lens to identify and *turn away* from those in rebellion to God.

The Sixth Bible Truth is turning away from everything against Jesus Christ protects us, prevents an economic collapse and secures our financial future, defends Christianity, and helps a greater number of people go to heaven instead of hell.

The people serving Jesus make the USA great, since they no longer do the devil's will. God says those who refuse to repent of their sins endanger the nation with the curse of *thou shalt not prosper in thy ways* (Deuteronomy 28:29 KJV). On the other hand, the Holy Bible shows that repenting ends economic troubles (2 Chronicles 7:13-14, Matthew 6:33).

To make the USA great, the Christian church, as the true leader of the nation under God, must unite and repent of sins. Not doing so means we live in darkness and lies, under Satan's power. Not repenting can result in an invasion or removal of the USA, as happened to Israel.

Sixth Bible Truth for protection and blessings 2 Tim. 3:5, 2 Chron. 15:8	Turn away from everything against Jesus Christ *Why? To love God and to heal our land.*

Every day we are to remember that God is holy. To have safety and God's favor, we must turn away from sin. To live in victory over sin the Bible says, *Submit yourselves therefore to God. Resist the devil, and he will flee from you.* (James 4:7 KJV).

If you agree with God for the USA to repent of sin, you are an American hero. Here are five major sins to repent of that cause God's judgment.

1. False gods - Other gods provoke the LORD to wrath, since forsaking Him is a covenant breaking act. As Christians, we know the Bible forbids turning to false religions and cults, such as Buddhists, Hindus, Muslims, Jehovah's Witnesses, Scientologists, and Mormons. Serving money instead of God is also a false god.

- "Thou shalt worship the LORD thy God, and Him only shalt thy serve" (Matthew 4:10)
- See Galatians 1:9, Matthew 6:24

Let's look at when Aaron the high priest and the Israelites made their own god, a molten calf, to go before them instead of the LORD. The people saw Moses was delayed in returning with God's instructions. Some thought Moses died, but he was seeking God for Israel's future (Exodus 32).

By not trusting in God and seeking deliverance another way, the people committed spiritual adultery to God. Aaron didn't stop the people from going astray with false gods, but misled them and fashioned a molten calf and said, *These be thy gods, O Israel, which brought thee up out of the land of Egypt* (Exodus 32:4 KJV). Then they celebrated their man-made god and caused shame with immorality and called this a feast unto the LORD.

They were breaking covenant, which provoked God. But Moses asked God to turn from His fierce wrath. Then Moses confronted Aaron and burned the molten calf in fire and ground it to powder; he scattered it on the water and made the Israelites drink it. God and Moses responded this way because other gods are God's enemies leading into darkness.

Moses told them they *sinned a great sin* (Exodus 32:30 KJV). To spare the people and families that would repent from the judgment for this sin, Moses made everyone make a decision, asking, *Who is on the LORD's side? let him come unto Me* (Exodus 32:26 KJV). God's response was to kill those who wouldn't follow Him and plague the people for their god. This serious response is because they forsook God.

From this example, we learn how God views His people turning to the world for help. We see that Moses didn't sin but did what God said and killed about 3,000 rebellious men. Some say this is harsh, but forsaking God meant everyone would have been destroyed and not enter the promised land.

Recall, today we don't kill those against God, but what we do is "turn away" from those who won't follow God.

The Bible Says Mormons Aren't Christians

To have God's protection, let's confess the great sin of thinking Mormons are Christians. One of the most common misconceptions that needs to be exposed to have God's healing is that Mormon's are perceived as Christians and "good people". But the Bible teaches Mormons are deceived and serve a false god (Matthew 4:10). Many people naively consider them to be Christians, but they are historically classified as a cult and forbidden by God for leadership since they turn our nation away from the LORD.

The following shows a comparison of Christianity with the Mormon cult.

	Christianity - *Truth*	Mormon Cult - *Error*
God	Always God eternally *Deut 33:27; Is. 43:10*	An exalted man; Mormons think God was first a man
Jesus Christ	Is God; Creator along with the Father and the Holy Spirit *Gen 1; John 1:1-3*	A created being, the spirit brother of Lucifer; Mormons have "another Jesus" *2 Cor. 11:4*
Holy Spirit	Is God; Comforter, Teacher, and Given to Christians *John 14:26*	Mormons have a "different spirit" not the Holy Spirit *2 Cor 11:4*
Holy Bible	God's Word, Final authority, Inerrant *2 Timothy 3:16-17*	Mormons have "another gospel" by adding to Scripture *2 Cor 11:4*
Salvation	Saved by grace through faith *Ephesians 2:8-9, John 3:16*	Saved by works and Mormonism
Man	Christians are children of God through faith in Jesus *John 1:12*	Exalted to become God and Godesses

Jesus Christ is God eternal and God's Son, but Mormons negate this and teach that Jesus is the spirit brother of Lucifer. The devil has never been on the same level as Jesus Christ. These lies are satanic in nature. What would you do if someone said your child is the spirit brother of Lucifer? You would tell them to leave and never come back.

Mormons also admit their founder had up to 40 wives, including a young 14 year old girl.[1] Due to their false teaching, Mormons were often chased out of town. The Mormon false god cannot save your soul or help the USA.

Some may think it doesn't matter who they voted for in 2012, but this and other times people voted for non-Christians must be confessed to restore God's protection. It is like Israel making a molten calf (Ezekiel 23, Exodus 32).

Recall, Israel suffered judgment from Saul's sin even after Saul died until David dealt with the sin (2 Samuel 21:1). There are popular ministers who associate with Glenn Beck and Mormons, and there are conservatives who would have been fine if Trump recommended Romney for Secretary of State.

Paul warned us not to receive those who preach another Jesus or another spirit or another gospel (2 Corinthians 11:4). He also taught, *If any man preach any other gospel unto you than that ye have received, let him be accursed* (Galatians 1:9 KJV). Should you vote for someone like that? If God says they are accursed, why would you want them in the White House, on a school board, or a political commentator?

This sin angers God. He says, *They have set up kings, but not by Me: they have made princes, and I knew it not... that they may be cut off* (Hosea 8:4 KJV). *Adulterers and adulteresses... friendship of the world is enmity with God... whosoever therefore will be a friend of the world is the enemy of God* (James 4:4 KJV). That is why trusting Romney and Beck backfired and made Obama stronger in 2012. Recall, leaders that hate the USA are judgment for turning to false gods.

The Word of God Is Above Ministers

How did our beloved USA go from seeing strange gods as sinful to turning to Mormons for help? The reason is ministers misled the people, which has caused judgment. This sin ahs caused part of the political corruption and other troubles. *The LORD plagued the people, because they made the calf, which Aaron made* (Exodus 32:35 KJV).

I am unaware of any minister mentioned here repenting, even though I asked them to. Look how common this sin is. Billy Graham hosted Romney in 2012 and said, "I'll do all I can to help you."[2] But God says, *If... any... bring not this doctrine, receive him not into your house, neither bid him God speed: For he that bid him God speed is partaker of his evil deeds* (2 John 10-11 KJV). This made evangelicals look weak in the media.[2]

The Billy Graham Evangelistic Association also removed listing Mormons from their website as a cult and misled the church with an article, "Can an Evangelical Christian Vote for a Mormon?"[2] The article told Christians, "The answer is yes" and that "God's principles" of voting for Romney cause "His blessing upon our nation"[2] even though God says to choose Christians and that turning to Romney causes God's wrath.

When asked if a Christian can vote for a Mormon, Franklin Graham said, "Yes, the fact that Mitt Romney is a Mormon doesn't bother me."[2] This is not a Christian statement. Both Graham's voting advice blocked the USA from having a Christian government that God blesses.

Joel Osteen said, "I see them [Mormons] as brothers in Christ" and when asked if it would be appropriate for Romney to speak at the largest Christian university (Liberty), Osteen replied, "It would be appropriate".[2] When questioned if a Mormon is a true Christian, Osteen answered, "In my mind they are."[2] This is the opposite of what the Bible teaches.

James Dobson has misled Christians with Romney since at least 2007 and shared, "I spent an hour and a half with him [Romney]. I liked him... he's still on the list".[2] Jerry Falwell Jr. had Romney and Beck speak to the Liberty student body.[2] Pat Roberston called Romney an "outstanding Christian".[2]

David Barton, John Hagee, TBN, Tony Perkins (Family Research Council), American Family Association (AFA), Kirk Cameron, Ray Comfort, Lou Engle, Rick Scarborough, Kenneth Copeland, Richard Land, Robert Jeffress, and others[5] either supported, or helped, Beck or Romney against Scripture.[2] Not one repented when I contacted their ministry.[3]

When asked if Obama was a Christian, Franklin Graham and Joel Osteen misled people to think Obama was a Christian even with Obama's support of Islam, abortion, sodomy, and lying. Osteen said, "I just believe in all my heart that [Obama] is a Christian."[2] Graham answered, Obama "has said that he is a Christian. Leave it at that."[2] But Jesus teaches that we *shall know them by their fruits* (Matthew 7:16 KJV). Also 1 John 2:4 states, *He who says, I know Him, and keeps not His commandments, is a liar, and the truth is not in him.*

To Have Protection, We Need Christian Leaders Who Follow God's Word

Remember that God calls those, who give an okay to vote for or associate with a Mormon or worldly people *adulterers*

(James 4:4 KJV) and He says they *played the harlot when she was Mine* (Ezekiel 23:5 KJV).

If we don't repent of helping God's enemies, how can He protect us from our enemies? *Because they have transgressed my covenant... the enemy shall pursue him* (Hosea 8:1-3 KJV).

Adultery to God is most dangerous. It gives God the right to destroy the USA, so we must ask for mercy. He sees voting for unbelievers as despising His Word, and He says this sin causes more terrorism (Leviticus 26:14-16). To have God's favor, we must find strong ministers, like the colonial pastors, who faithfully teach the Gospel to only have Christian leaders.

Even ministers who evangelize, fight for pro-life, call for liberty, give Christmas gifts to children, pray and fast, teach on miracles, and oppose Islam commit adultery if they support Mormons or worldly people.

Honestly, I felt let down by these ministers and you may feel that they betrayed your trust, but God says to trust in Him not people. To be saved and walk with God all you have to do is follow Jesus and the Bible. By trusting in Jesus for salvation and studying God's Word daily, you will keep your soul safe. I encourage you to pray, *Father, my loyalty is to You and to Your Word, the Holy Bible. In Jesus' name. Amen.*

Many voters wonder why God did not remove Obama for eight years. But God waits for them to be honest about the sin of not crying out for Christian leaders. God says, *none shall rescue him. I will go and return to my place, till they acknowledge their offence, and seek my face* (Hosea 5:14-15 KJV).

What prevented God from destroying our nation for Democrats and Republicans turning to God's enemies? The answer I find in Scripture is those who wanted a Christian government and obeyed God by refusing to sin by voting for unbelievers, just as when Moses saved Israel by not compromising with the gold calf (Exodus 32).

The LORD is a jealous God. Not repenting of adultery is serious. In the Old Testament those who led people away from the LORD and to other gods were killed to stop God's wrath (Exodus 32:27, Deuteronomy 13, Leviticus 25). Israel's enemies defeated Israel until Joshua removed the accursed people when Israel transgressed covenant by taking an accursed thing (Joshua 7:1-12). Today, as the New Testament teaches, we just turn away from false teachers and those not repenting (James 4:4, 2 Timothy 3:5).

This is a good time to ask God's forgiveness for turning to Mormons for help instead of God's people. Pray: *Father, You are the one true God. We ask You to forgive the USA for turning to Mormons and other false ways in politics and elsewhere. We trust in You. In Jesus' name. Amen.*

All strange gods are forbidden. The lie of universalism, which is when people think that everyone goes to heaven, is sin too. The only way to go to heaven is to believe in Jesus Christ to save you. But some ministers imply that Muslims and/or Mormons and/or atheists go to heaven. This is false teaching. Jesus says, *I am the way, the truth, and the life. No one comes to the Father except through Me* (John 14:6 KJV).

Divide Politics as Christian and Heathen
Rather Than Right and Left

American Center Political Chart

Where does your politician fit?

SECULAR
"LIBERTARIAN"
Motive: Self
Duty: Serve Self
Rights: Man Made
Gov.: Leads to Anarchy
God: Ignores God
Wars: Defensive but Godless
Economy: Free Market Attempt

TEA PARTY

AMERICAN †
Like founding fathers
Motive: Advance the Kingdom of our Lord
Jesus Christ & Enjoy the Liberties of the Gospel
Duty: Serve God
Rights: God-given: Life, Liberty, Pursuit
of Happiness, Property, Conscience
Gov.: Christian Republic
God: The LORD
War: Defensive, Just Cause
Economy: God Blessed Abundance

On the LORD's Side
God's blesses

LEFT (Liberal)
Motive: Oppose Conservatives
Duty: Serve Government
Rights: Government-given
Gov.: Socialist
God: Anti-Christian
Wars: Aggressive
Economy: Debt-based

RIGHT (Conservative)
Motive: Oppose Liberals
Duty: Serve Big Business
Rights: Big Business-given
Gov.: Democracy
God: Any god (i.e. Mormon cult)
Wars: Aggressive
Economy: Debt-based

PROGRESSIVE

COMMUNIST
Motive: Fear
Duty: Serve Dictator
Rights: None (Police State)
Gov.: Dictator
God: Attack God
Wars: Unjust
Economy: Communist Slave

Shaded areas are
responsible for God's Judgment
"Enemy of God" James 4:4
UnAmerican and Extremist

Moderate combines *Left* and *Right*

We must repent of another sin. The devil is scheming to remove Christianity from politics by getting people to say they are "left" or "right" instead of Christian or non-Christian. When we examine it, being a "liberal" or a "conservative" are unAmerican. By choosing a side we turn away from Jesus and choose how we want to sin. God sees people as either Christian or heathen, not "conservative" or "liberal".

Neither the "left" or "right" represent America. This chart shows God's will for politics and how far from our founders the "left" and "right" are. President Trump is a significant improvement and is approximately on the edge of being a true American. However, Obama and Clinton would be the farthest away from a real American.

President Trump can easily be like our Christian founders. He needs to fear God more and: (1) Insist to have Christian religious liberty as the USA's top priority, while renouncing false gods (Mark 12:30, Deuteronomy 8:19); (2) Agree with our founders that God says homosexuals and transgenders are "wicked and sinners before the LORD exceedingly" and sin is what provokes God. (Genesis 13:13); and (3) Stand up more for the Fourth Amendment and oppose spying on innocent Americans.

Even though there have been unproven allegations against him from forty years ago, an example of someone with a modern day, true American public service record is Roy Moore. Consistently, Moore has shown the good fruit of believing "the LORD is our lawgiver" (Isaiah 33:22); he was removed from office for refusing to remove a Ten Commandments display! He also boldly stands for God-given rights, traditional marriage, and being pro-life. Whereas, many civil servants don't even know what God-given rights are.

Some try to justify voting "left" or "right" as the lesser of two evils, but God says turning to unbelievers is a sin that endangers our lives (2 Corinthians 6:14-18). It is like saying, "I voted for Baal not Molech," or a child saying, "Dad, I stole $9 instead of $10." The devil uses "left" and "right" to deceive Christians, who give millions of dollars to organizations endorsing God's enemies, whether it is pro-life, marriage, family, or other groups. But God wants us to financially support those who only promote Christians.

2. Homosexual sin - God is for the marriage of one man and one woman for a lifetime, and doing this brings us God's safety. The truth is Jesus Christ makes families strong. That means we are to turn from sexual sins, including fornication, adultery, and sodomy. The Bible says:

- "Be not deceived: neither fornicators... nor adulterers, nor effeminate, nor abusers of themselves with mankind... shall inherit the kingdom of God" (1 Corinthians 6:9-10 KJV).

Since God will destroy the USA if people rebel against Him with same-sex marriage, we must look at this further. Remember, God says:

- "God gave them up unto vile affections: for even their women did change the natural use into that which is against nature: And likewise also the men, leaving the natural use of the woman, burned in their lust one toward another; men with men..." (Romans 1:26-27 KJV).

- God turning the cities of Sodom and Gomorrah "into ashes condemned them with an overthrow, making them an ensample unto those that after should live ungodly" (2 Peter 2:6 KJV).

- "The men of Sodom were wicked and sinners before the LORD exceedingly" (Genesis 13:13 KJV).
- See Romans 1:24-32, Leviticus 18:22 & 25, and Jude 7

Our national security is very important. God says, *When the host goeth forth against thine enemies, then keep thee from every wicked thing* (Deuteronomy 23:9 KJV). With sodomy and other sins in the military, God doesn't go with them. That puts our nation at stake. Will you let God know you are on His side and oppose sin?

The LORD is our Lawgiver and Judge, so we must follow Him. Same-sex marriage is much more than sexual sin; it is defying God who created male and female.

HOLY BIBLE Bible Principle

Everyone loves and everyone hates. Do you love God and hate sin? Or do you love sin and hate God?

Jesus said, *He that has my commandments, and keeps them, he it is that loves me* (John 14:21). Those who follow God are *lovers of God* (2 Timothy 3:4 KJV). Yet, sodomites call Christians, including our founders, "haters" and "bigots" for loving God. However, God's Word calls homosexuals and other sinners "haters of God," since they oppose Him (Romans 1:30 KJV).

The truth is everyone loves and everyone hates. We either love God and hate sin, or we love sin and hate God. Light and darkness can not coexist. What kind of lover are you? Do you love God or sin? What type of hater are you? Do you hate sin or God? If you want to go to heaven, then love God. He says,

That they all might be damned who believed not the truth, but had pleasure in unrighteousness (2 Thessalonians 2:12 KJV).

The Bible says the ungodly are at war with God. Jesus Christ explains why, *For everyone that does evil hates the light* (John 3:20). Liberals, who hate God, discriminated against and fired the CEO of Mozilla for supporting traditional marriage. That is why "hate crime laws" are corrupt. "Hate crime laws" were invented to bully everyone who follows God.

In his popular dictionary, Noah Webster defined sodomy using Romans 1 as "A crime against nature." For God to bless the military, Washington, the most respected American, court martialed sodomites and had, "Abhorrence and Detestation of such Infamous Crimes."[4] Since "hate crime laws" would put in jail God and the founding fathers, it is obvious these "laws" are unBiblical and unAmerican. The USA either does God's will like our founders say to do with laws against sin and God blesses our lives, or the nation opposes God and is cursed.

Scientifically, research show greater health issues with sodomites. The CDC reports that two in five homosexuals have HIV and get 57% of the new HIV cases,[5] and studies show their average age of death is between 39 - 43 years old.[6]

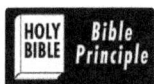

HOLY BIBLE *Bible Principle*

Pastors asking people to repent makes the USA great again.

What is the most Christ-like and compassionate response to sodomites and other sinners? Jesus Christ shows us. He said, *Repent ye, and believe in the Gospel* (Mark 1:15 KJV). He loves people and wants each of us to go to heaven instead of hell.

If the shamefulness of sodomy doesn't bother a person, it is a sign of becoming "a reprobate" (Romans 1:28 KJV), unapproved by God. Right away, that person must confess the sin, receive forgiveness by Jesus' blood, and cry out to God to fill them with the Holy Spirit, so they don't lose their soul.

God and the Constitution: Same-sex Marriage is Not law

Above all, the USA must obey the Word of God, which commands, *Thou shalt not lie with mankind, as with womankind: it is abomination* (Leviticus 18:22 KJV). God tells us same-sex marriage is not law. Then we follow the Constitution. Our founders wrote it and know what is constitutional. To do God's will they made homosexual sin illegal in all 13 colonies, as did all 50 states.

Exercising our God-given right to freedom of Christian speech is guaranteed by the Bible and the Bill of Rights. We need every pastor to stand up for God's law, and then the law of the land, and say same-sex marriage is disobeying God and the Constitution.

Like our founding fathers, Mike Huckabee boldly defined it as "judicial tyranny" to jail Kim Davis because a high school civics class knows the Supreme Court can't make a law. Remember, the Constitution dictates that laws are made by congress and executed by the president.[7] Moreover, congress can't make a law against God, because the First Amendment says, *Congress shall make no law... prohibiting the free exercise [of Christianity]*. We are to always remember that laws against Christians are illegal!

Just think how many people end up in hell by homosexual marriage, including young people learning sinful ways in schools. After all, no one can change God's ordinance of marriage (James 4:4, Romans 1:24-32, Isaiah 24:5).

To stop God from destroying the USA for defying Him, we must pray and work for Christian leaders to replace those who hate God. He shows us how to respond to same-sex marriage. To establish law and order and restore God's protection, we and our churches are to:

- Cry out to Him to deliver us from the tyranny (Judges 3:9, 2 Corinthians 6:14-18).
- Boldly say the USA obeys God rather than men.
- Teach it is illegal to make a law against Christianity.

Remember, lives are at stake. To defend Christianity, pastors must preach to repent of sin. When was the last time your pastor taught to repent of these major sins? As it was in 1776, it is today. Bold pastors and Christians who insist that our nation serves Jesus Christ bring God's favor to us.

In summary, reasons to do God's will on marriage are:

- **To love God** - Our duty is to obey God's will of one man and one woman marriage (Matthew 19:4-6).
- **To go to Heaven** - God saved Lot who was vexed by the sin of the sodomites. But Lot's wife didn't fear God and lost her soul to hell where the worm shall not die and the fire is not quenched (2 Peter 2:6-9).
- **To save the USA** - God is to be feared. He promises that same-sex marriage means certain destruction of the country (Jude 7, 2 Peter 2:6, Leviticus 18:25).

3. Abortion - God is pro-life. That is why the USA is pro-life. He promises to heal our land by our nation repenting from shedding innocent blood. In its most base form, abortion is simply murder.

- "Thou shalt not kill" (Matthew 5:21 KJV)
- "They sacrificed their sons and their daughters unto devils, and shed innocent blood" (Psalm 106:37 KJV).

When politicians promote sacrificing our children by spending about $1.5 billion in three years to abortion related companies, they break covenant and use our money against our consciences.[8] Our Christian duty is to never have government funded abortion and to bring back the ban on abortions to make the USA great again This will stop more innocent blood crying out to God, which results in leaders who hate Americans as God's judgment. This sin is a curse that is causing so many of the USA's problems (Psalm 106:37-42).

Here is hope. If you had an abortion or if you have guilt from another sin, ask God to cleanse your conscience with Jesus Christ's blood. God will remove the guilt (Hebrews 9:14). Jesus' blood will make you whole.

4. The Occult – Many are unaware of the dangers of Satan's darkness, but the devil uses movies, books, schools, social media, and other sources to influence people with familiar spirits, psychics, talking to the dead, sorcery, numerology, fortune telling, horoscopes, meditation with demons, and witches.

- "There shall not be found among you any one that maketh his son or his daughter to pass through the fire, or that useth divination, or an observer of times, or an enchanter, or a witch, or a charmer, or a consulter with familiar spirits, or a wizard, or a necromancer. For all that do these things are an abomination unto the LORD" (Deuteronomy 18:10-12 KJV).

5. The Lie of Separation of Church and State – There is an important message that pastors and Christians must teach and take action on to make the USA exceptional. We must declare our country follows the LORD and work for a government like our founders that gladly submits to the authority of God. Separation of church and state is:

1. Not what our founders or the USA practiced
2. Not Constitutional
3. Not historical
4. Sin that endangers the country's survival

The Word of God shows that government is to submit to God and recognize His sovereignty:

- "For the LORD is our judge, the LORD is our lawgiver, the LORD is our king" (Isaiah 33:22 KJV)
- "The government shall be upon his shoulder" (Isaiah 9:6 KJV)
- "Be wise now therefore, O ye kings: be instructed, ye judges of the earth. Serve the LORD with fear, and rejoice with trembling. Kiss the Son, lest he be angry, and ye perish from the way, when his wrath is kindled but a little. Blessed are all they that put their trust in him." (Psalm 2:10-12 KJV)

The good news is that times of refreshing come by repenting of everything against Jesus Christ.

Next, we will learn the hope of God's total forgiveness.

✝ Prayer

Father, I and the USA are on Your side. We repent of everything against Jesus Christ, including tolerance of other

gods, turning to the heathen, abortion, homosexuality, the occult, and the lie of separation of church and state.
In Jesus' name. Amen.

✔️ Reflection Questions

1. *God calls us to repent of all sin. What are the major sins in this chapter that greatly endanger our nation's safety?*
2. *Explain why turning from sin makes the USA great?*
3. *What will you and your church do to help others repent and have victory over sin?*

9

Seventh Truth—God's Mercy and Forgiveness

"You are a gracious God, and merciful,
slow to anger, and of great kindness."
Jonah 4:2 KJV

It is not too late for the USA to receive God's mercy and forgiveness for our national sins. Why does God want to show mercy to the USA? He knows we need mercy for our great sins so our nation is not destroyed. False gods, same-sex marriage, and selling innocent aborted babies' body parts grieve the Holy Spirit. But God's mercy is greater than our sins.

We must confess our sins to God and be forgiven. This gives us hope and a new beginning.

To the woman caught in adultery Jesus Christ said, *Neither do I condemn thee: go, and sin no more* (John 8:11 KJV). No one deserves forgiveness. We cannot earn it, or buy it. Yet, by putting our faith in Jesus for forgiveness we are forgiven.

God is Satisfied with the Sacrifice of Jesus

As the Lamb of God, Jesus laid down His life for us to redeem us from our sins, the innocent for the guilty. *For He hath made him to be sin for us, who knew no sin; that we might be made the righteousness of God in him* (2 Corinthians 5:21 KJV).

Seventh Bible Truth for protection and blessings 1 John 1:7, Jonah 4:2	Restore the Cross and pray to receive forgiveness for the USA's sins by the sacrifice of Jesus *Why? To restore God's favor and to live in grace.*

The curses from sin are removed by: (1) Atonement for our personal and national sins by Jesus Christ on the cross; and (2) Asking God to be forgiven. So the next Bible Truth has two parts: the cross brings back God's favor (atonement) and when we ask for forgiveness, then we live in God's grace.

The Seventh Bible Truth is restoring the cross and praying to receive forgiveness for the USA's sins by the sacrifice of Jesus will restore God's favor and grace to our lives and nation. Each of us and the USA are on the LORD's side when we believe that Jesus Christ's death on the cross forgives our sins.

Without Jesus there is no way to have God's favor. We are going to be forgiven and remove God's judgment now. Perhaps, the reason that Judah was destroyed after Josiah is because there was no atonement for Manasseh's sins. That is why we need to cleanse the USA from the sins of Obama and others. We don't want to share in their curse.

Restoring the altar of the LORD is part of what King Asa did to end judgment (2 Chronicles 15:8). When God plagued Israel during King David's time, David built an altar to God and prayed and the plague ended (2 Samuel 24:25).

God remembers our covenant through Jesus who took God's wrath for our sins on the cross. Jesus is the altar, priest, and victim. That is why we put our faith in our Lord dying on the cross for us to restore the altar today. Restoring the Cross brings Heaven on earth—for you personally and for the USA.

Remember, Calvary's tree is God's answer to the analogy of the bricks falling and the sycamore tree being cut down in *The Harbinger* book. These *7 Bible Truths* give us the answer.

When Jesus forgave our sins on the cross, He was sealing and keeping covenant. His blood is the blood of the covenant. *The blood of Jesus Christ his Son cleanseth us from all sin* (1 John 1:7 KJV). *He... put away sin by the sacrifice of Himself* (Hebrews 9:26 KJV).

HOLY BIBLE Bible Principle

The church receives forgiveness for the USA.

The blood of Jesus is more powerful than any sin. The nail prints Jesus has from the three nails when they crucified Him proves He loves us and paid the price for our sins. To be forgiven of your sins, pray: *Father, I confess my sins of ___. I am cleansed by Jesus Christ's blood. In Jesus' name. Amen.*

Pray and Receive Forgiveness for the USA

Do you feel sorrowful for our nation's sins. Our consciences are to convict us that it is shameful for boys to enter girls dressing rooms at schools and for teachers to have students read about the occult. The sins of our land stand out. God expects us to weep and wail over them (James 4:9). They will either be forgiven by Jesus, or the USA will be punished.

The restoration of God's favor, by the cross and the blood of Jesus symbolized, ended the plague that killed 14,700 people because of the rebellion of Korah (Numbers 16:46-50).

Acknowledging the cross as a nation and humbling ourselves in covenant prayer to receive forgiveness for the country's sins make the USA great. On the other hand, ignoring Jesus' death and refusing to ask for forgiveness results in a curse and greatly endangers the nation.

To restore jobs, have liberty, get out of debt, remove terrorism, and protect our environment, we must ask for forgiveness (1 John 1:9, 2 Chronicles 7:14). Let's approach God in prayer with holy reverence.

Next, we will fully restore God's blessings.

✝ Prayer to Forgive the USA's Sins

Father,

You are merciful. The USA restores the cross. With godly sorrow Americans ask for Your mercy for our sins instead of Your judgment. John 8:11, Jonah 4:2, Amos 5:18

The USA confesses and repents of:

- *Other gods Matthew 4:10*
- *Homosexuality, adultery and fornication Jude 7, 1 Corinthians 6:9-10*
- *Not having Christian religious liberty as our priority as a nation Mark 12:30*

- *The places we don't follow Jesus in government, schools, courts and the military, and taking the Holy Bible & Christian prayer out of schools* 2 Timothy 2:12, Isaiah 59:21
- *Not demanding our God-given rights of life, liberty, the pursuit of happiness, property, and conscience* Genesis 1:27, Acts 5:29
- *Helping the wicked instead of supporting Christians in politics and business* 2 Timothy 3:5, 2 Chronicles 19:2, 2 Corinthians 6:14-18
- *Abortion* Matthew 5:17
- *Unjust wars* Mark 12:31
- *Coveting* Matthew 6:24, Ephesians 5:5
- *Occult, sorcery, and witchcraft* Deuteronomy 18:10-12
- *All other sins* 2 Chronicles 7:14

We receive forgiveness for our personal and national sins by the sacrifice of Jesus. 1 John 1:7 & 9

In Jesus' name. Amen.

✓ Reflection Questions

1. *What is the meaning of 1 John 1:7?*
2. *Are you confident your sins are forgiven? Why?*
3. *Why does asking God to forgive the USA give you safety and improve the economy?*

10

Covenant Protection, Blessings, and Favor

"Blessed is the nation whose God is the LORD..."
Psalm 33:12 KJV

We have learned that God wants us to give Him our hearts re-affirming: The LORD is the God of the USA and Americans are His people. Insisting to have Christian religious liberty with our *One Nation Under God* covenant relationship is what makes America great.

By learning the *7 Bible Truths*, we can now fully live them out. We are going to seal our covenant, so prepare your heart before God because this is holy. As Jesus Christ purchased our salvation with His blood, He purchased the USA to be His covenant Christian nation. Because God gives Americans everything in covenant, will you let Him know that you submit yourself and the USA entirely to Him?

Kings Asa and Josiah rejoiced to covenant with God when they recognized Judah was in danger for their sin.

7 BIBLE TRUTHS TO HAVE PROTECTION AND SAVE THE USA

First Bible Truth Psalm 33:12, 2 Cor. 6:18	Re-affirm Covenant: The LORD is the God of the USA and Americans are His people Why? To get the USA in right relationship with God.
Second Bible Truth 2 Chron. 15:12, Matt. 7:7	Seek God with all your heart and all your soul Why? To find and His Help.
Third Bible Truth Luke 6:47-49, 2 Chron. 34:31	Obey the Holy Bible with all your heart and all your soul Why? To do God's will.
Fourth Bible Truth Isaiah 33:22, Phil. 2:11	Have no king but King Jesus Why? Jesus brings the Kingdom of God's blessings, including protection and liberty.
Fifth Bible Truth Matt. 28:19-20, Is. 59:21	Make disciples of the USA Why? To raise godly generations.
Sixth Bible Truth 2 Tim. 3:5, 2 Chron. 15:8	Turn away from everything against Jesus Christ Why? To love God.
Seventh Bible Truth 1 John 1:7, Jonah 4:2	Restore the Cross and receive forgiveness for the USA's sins by the sacrifice of Jesus Why? To restore God's favor and to live in grace.

The *7 Bible Truths* are the American breakthrough secret that always works. The only way to protect the next generations is for them to walk with Jesus Christ. Covenant gives us confidence to have Americanism, not globalism.

Unfortunately, we were taught to be politically correct and that false religions were to be present in our schools, military, and government. Then those outside of covenant tried to take our Christian faith away which led to the great judgments and even the danger of a final judgment. But we hold fast and say no! The LORD is the God of the USA!

Will You Join Covenant?

The Jamestown Settlers, Pilgrims, and others show us how a few people by faith can turn a heathen land to be the strongest Christian nation ever. Now, we must work to make the USA the greatest Christian nation ever. Here are questions to ask yourself to see if you love God and country:

7 Questions to Seal the USA's Covenant with God

1. Do I publicly say: The LORD is the God of the USA and Americans are His people?
2. Am I seeking God with all my heart and all my soul, including for our nation?
3. Do I speak up for the USA to obey the Holy Bible?
4. Am I living with Jesus as King of the USA?
5. Will I help make disciples of our nation?
6. Do I speak up for our nation to turn away from everything against Jesus Christ?
7. Have I restored the cross and prayed to receive forgiveness for the USA's sins by Jesus' blood?

If you answer yes to these questions, you are on the LORD's side and He invites you to join covenant. You must agree to be in covenant. As you get ready to pray, thank the LORD that He is our God. Then examine yourself if there is any sin you can confess to God. By sealing covenant the devil's works are destroyed (1 John 3:8). Like our founders, we join God and country together forever. Americans love God!

✝ Covenant Prayer

To re-affirm covenant, pray and sign the following prayer. As an individual, family, or church, you may want to take communion as this is a holy covenant through Jesus Christ.

Protect Yourself and Save the USA
Pray and Live: The USA's Covenant with God   ✝▓▓

Father,

You are holy. We thank You that the USA is dedicated to You in covenant to all generations.

LORD, You are the God of the USA and Americans are Your people. We seek You and obey the Holy Bible with all our hearts and all our souls. Jesus is our King, so our nation makes Christian disciples and we turn away from everything against Jesus Christ.

To do Your will, the USA agrees with You that marriage is one man and one woman only, the Bible is to be read in schools with Christian prayer, and abortion is to be banned again. We work for covenant Christian nation leaders to immediately replace those disobeying You.

We thank You for the Cross and by Jesus' blood we receive forgiveness for the USA's sins.

In Jesus' name. Amen.

_____
Your Name

We make the USA secure and strong when we let God know that we agree with Him and not the Supreme Court's rebellious, anti-God opinions, including same-sex marriage, removing our founder's Christianity from schools, abortion, and separation of church and state. These covenant breaking acts, along with false gods and voting for unbelievers, endanger our loved ones and nation with God's judgment.

You can print and put *The USA's Covenant with God* on your refrigerator, by your desk, and inside your church or ministry's bulletins to re-affirm it often. You can also take a picture of it to save and share it. On the second Sunday of each month, join our nation in praying our covenant to make the USA great. At my website, www.USA.church, there are free resources to use in your home, church, work, and school.

Now, let's live the real American Dream *to advance the Kingdom of our Lord Jesus Christ and to enjoy the liberties of the Gospel in purity and peace.*[1] While we have work to do to be exceptional throughout the nation in our families, education, business, and churches, we know re-affirming and daily living this covenant gives us God's protection and prosperity. Together, let's do all we can for God and country. By following Jesus, the USA is great!

✅ Reflection Questions

1. *How does covenant with God give you hope?*
2. *Why does Jesus make the USA great?*
3. *Who can you and your church invite to join covenant?*

೧೯೪

Thank you for reading this inspirational book to bring God's protection, strength, and prosperity to your life and the nation. The next steps to help make the USA great are to seek God how you can share:

- SAVE AMERICA
- **The 7 Bible Truths**

I invite you and your church to join:

- **One Million Americans on the LORD's Side**™
- The American Disciple Making Team™
- The Daily Biblical Prayer for Government™
- Wednesdays: Nationwide Prayer and Fasting™
- Christians Uniting to Save the USA™

Sign up at www.USA.church

Resource: Understanding Blessings and Judgment

God gives blessings for obedience and judgment for disobedience. Here is a list of major Biblical judgments.

"They That Hate You Shall Reign Over You"

Overview: God wants us to have good leaders that care for our well being and ensure our liberty. We have peace of mind and live in freedom when we have quality representatives.

Key Bible Verse: *...if your soul abhor my judgments, so that ye will not do all my commandments, but that ye break my covenant: I also will do this unto you... they that hate you shall reign over you* (Leviticus 26:14-17 KJV).

Judgment: Bad leaders who act against the people are from national disobedience of God's Word and covenant breaking acts, such as praying to false gods, abortion, and the people who say the USA is not a Christian nation.

Examples: Corrupt leaders: oppose God-given rights, do not listen to the people, violate the Constitution, act as tyrants, commit treason, favor foreigners, and say bad things about the USA and our Christian founders. Includes: anti-American ways, big government, communism, socialism, the New World Order, regulations opposing our liberty, forcing GMO foods, and omitting references to God.

Blessing: God gives good leaders when we:
- Obey God's Word in our lives and government.
  - Separate from the heathen and their sin,
  - Ban abortion, and
  - Think about holy things (Psalm 106:34-42).
- Re-affirm covenant: The USA's God is the LORD.

Additional Bible Background:

- See: Psalm 106:35-42, Isaiah 19:4 & 42:24, Ezekiel 23:28-30, Leviticus 26:40-41, and Judges 2:11-4:2.
- *We are servants... for the land that thou gavest unto our fathers... it yieldeth much increase unto the kings whom thou hast set over us because of our sins: also they have dominion over our bodies, and over our cattle, at their pleasure, and we are in great distress.* (Nehemiah 9:36-37 KJV).
- *I will... deliver thee into the hand of brutish men, and skilful to destroy* (Ezekiel 21:31 KJV).
- *I will bring the worst of the heathen* (Ezekiel 7:24 KJV).
- *The LORD shall bring a nation against thee... whose tongue thou shalt not understand; A nation of fierce countenance, which shall not regard the person of the old, nor shew favour to the young:* (Deuteronomy 28:49-50 KJV).
- Turning to the ungodly results in them turning on us (Ezekiel 16:36-37, Nahum 3:5).

Foreigners Rising Higher and Taking Jobs Away

Foreigners Rising Higher and Taking Jobs Away

Overview: God expects His Christian nation to keep covenant with Him and be separate from the world (Psalm 106:35-42). We have national sovereignty, unity, and more jobs when we put America first. This gives safety and security.

Key Bible Verse: *...if thou wilt not hearken unto the voice of the LORD thy God... The fruit of thy land, and all thy* *labours, shall a nation which thou knowest not eat up; and thou shalt be only oppressed and crushed alway... The stranger that is within thee shall get up above thee very high; and thou shalt come down very low.* (Deuteronomy 28:15, 33, 43 KJV).

Judgment: Foreigners taking away jobs and bringing anti-Christian ways to the USA are God's judgment. How can we be safe with an open border allowing in enemies, gangs, disease, terrorists, and those against our Christian nation?

Examples: An unprotected, open border. Illegal aliens. Bad leaders and courts working to bring Muslims terrorists to the USA. Releasing illegal aliens who committed crimes to the public. Banning American flags.

Additional Bible Background:

- *The bloody city... full of lies and robbery... because of the multitude of the whoredoms... witchcrafts... the gates of thy land shall be set wide open unto thine enemies* (Nahum 3:13 KJV).
- See: Leviticus 26:38.

Blessing: If we want the USA blessed and to stop losing jobs to foreigners, then we must:

- Obey the Holy Bible, personally and as a nation.
- Be truthful and honest.
- Repent of taking things from others.
- Serve the LORD only.
- Renounce witchcraft. (Nahum 3:1-13)

Terrorism

Overview: We can have God's protection and live safe lives free of terror. This is God's desire.

Key Bible Verse: *If... ye will not do all My commandments, but that ye break My covenant: I also will do this unto you; I will even appoint over you terror* (Leviticus 26:14-16 KJV).

Judgment: The judgment of terror is caused by the nation disobeying God's Word and covenant breaking acts, such as political leaders praying with other gods, voting for the ungodly, the people who say the USA is not a Christian nation, not acknowledging that Jesus is King of the USA, same-sex marriage, etc...

Examples: 9-11, Muslim/ISIS attacks, San Bernardino...

Blessing: The way to defeat terrorism is to:

- Follow the Word of God, personally and as a nation, with laws based on the Holy Bible.
- Pray to the LORD and not to false gods.
- Agree that Jesus Christ is Lord of the USA.
- Have schools read the Bible again.

Additional Bible Background:

- The full terror judgment is being slain by enemies and fleeing when no one pursues (Leviticus 26:17).

Captivity, Invasion, or Destruction

Overview: God is faithful and protects those in covenant, but He gives a final judgment when wickedness is too great.

Key Bible Verses: *If thou do at all forget the LORD thy God, and walk after other gods, and serve them, and worship them... ye shall surely perish.* (Deuteronomy 8:19 KJV).

Sodom and Gomorrha... giving themselves over to fornication, and going after strange flesh, are set forth for an example, suffering the vengeance of eternal fire (Jude 7 KJV).

Judgment: Captivity, invasion, or destruction are from turning to false gods (Mormons, Muslims, Buddhists...) and forsaking the LORD by trusting in the ungodly for help. Destruction is the judgment for homosexual and transgender sin, and is also the judgment for widespread corruption.

Examples: Communist ways (a beginning type of captivity). Israel being invaded. Sodom and Gomorrah destroyed. The flood destroying everything, but those in Noah's ark.

Blessing: To avoid a final destruction the USA is to:
- Pray to the LORD only and not to strange gods.
- Agree with God that marriage is one man and one woman only, and that homosexual, transgender, and other sexual immorality are sins.
- Live a holy life to please God and repent of wickedness.

Additional Bible Background:
- *See also: 2 Peter 2:6, Romans 1:24-32.*

- *But the men of Sodom were wicked and sinners before the LORD exceedingly (Genesis 13:13 KJV).*
- Homosexual, transgender, and other sexual sins are abominations that the land vomits out the inhabitants for (Leviticus 18:22 & 18:25, Deuteronomy 22:5).
- *They forsook the LORD God of their fathers, which brought them out of the land of Egypt, and followed other gods... He sold them into the hands of their enemies* (Judges 2:12-14 KJV)
- *For all the evil abominations... they shall fall by the sword...* (Ezekiel 6:11 KJV)
- Unbelievers persecuting Christians is from God's people turning to them in business and politics. *She was mine; and she doted on her lovers... Wherefore I have delivered her into the hand of her lovers* (Ezekiel 23:5, 9 KJV); The full judgment is to be taken captive and killed (Ezekiel 16:38-41) .

Economic Loss, Spoiling, Debt, and High Taxes

Overview: If we want prosperity and financial security, then we must end God's judgment on our economy. This matters, as having additional money is a benefit to our lives.

Key Bible Verse: They *rejected His statutes, and His covenant that He made with their fathers... they... went after the heathen... and worshipped all the host of heaven... they caused their sons and their daughters to pass through the fire, and used divination... Therefore the LORD... delivered them into the hand of spoilers* (2 Kings 17:15-20 KJV).

147

Judgment: High taxes, the national debt, and losing money through spoiling are Biblical signs that we are being judged.

Examples: The nation not prospering. Lower paying jobs, fewer middle class households, and poverty. Government, businesses, or foreigners taking our wealth by high taxes, debts, housing market crashes, and other financial losses.

Blessings: To have God give us abundance, He says to:

- Follow the Word of God, personally and as a nation with laws based on the Holy Bible.
- Be loyal to our founders' covenant and faithfully say the USA is a Christian nation.
- Choose God-fearing leaders.
- Stop tolerating false gods in the USA.
- Ban abortion again.
- Repent of the occult, witchcraft, and the devil's ways.

Additional Bible Background:

- *You shall not prosper in your ways* (Deuteronomy 28:29).
- *They shall lend to thee, and thou shalt not lend to him* (Deuteronomy 28:44 KJV).
- *They... followed other gods... of the people that were round about them... And the anger of the LORD was hot against Israel, and He delivered them into the hands of spoilers that spoiled them, and He sold them into the hands of their enemies... so that they could not any longer stand before their enemies* (Judges 2:12-14 KJV).
- God reverses things when we repent (Judges 2:16-18).
- *Seek ye first the kingdom of God, and his righteousness; and all these things shall be added unto you* (Matthew 6:33 KJV).

- Drought, bad crops, pestilence, and widespread business failure are God's judgment (Deuteronomy 28:15 & 40, 2 Samuel 21:1).
- *Alas for all the evil abominations of the house of Israel! for they shall fall by the sword, by the famine, and by the pestilence.* (Ezekiel 6:11 KJV)
- *If I shut up heaven that there be no rain, or if I command the locusts to devour... or if I send pestilence... If My people, which are called by My name, shall humble themselves, and pray, and seek My face, and turn from their wicked ways; then will I hear from heaven, and will forgive their sin, and will heal their land* (2 Chronicles 7:13-14 KJV).

Harm to the Earth and Animals

Overview: The only way to protect creation is for our country to turn from our sins. Great devastation to the environment comes by God's judgment.

Key Bible Verses: *And GOD saw that the wickedness of man was great in the earth, and that every imagination of the thoughts of his heart was only evil continually... And the LORD said, I will destroy man whom I have created from the face of the earth; both man, and beast, and the creeping thing, and the fowls of the air; for it repenteth me that I have made them. (Genesis 6:5-7 KJV).*

Then the LORD rained upon Sodom and upon Gomorrah brimstone and fire from the LORD out of heaven; And he overthrew those cities, and all the plain, and all the inhabitants of the cities, and that which grew upon the ground (Genesis 19:24-25 KJV).

Judgment: The Bible teaches the judgment of devastation to the environment is caused by wickedness, rebellion to God, thinking on evil, and homosexual sin (Genesis 6:5-17; 19:24-28, Exodus 7:14-11:10).

Examples: Much of the harm to the earth and animals today is caused by sin. The world in Noah's day was destroyed except for those in the ark. Sodom and Gomorrah were destroyed. Egypt's plagues ruined many things.

Blessings: To protect the earth and animals, we must:

- Repent as a nation of wickedness, evil thoughts, rebellion to God, and homosexual and other sins.

Additional Bible Background:

- *... because there is no truth, nor mercy, nor knowledge of God in the land. By swearing, and lying, and killing, and stealing, and committing adultery... Therefore shall the land mourn, and every one that dwelleth therein shall languish, with the beasts of the field, and with the fowls of heaven; yea, the fishes of the sea also shall be taken away. (Hosea 4:1-3 KJV)*

- But the Holy Spirit gives life to creation when we follow God.

- The Bible says the priority is to live a holy life, instead of focusing on the environment and being "green". That will best protect the earth and animals. We are to fear God, for He controls the climate, not man; He has promised to not destroy the earth, but He judges the people sinning (Genesis 8:22).

Resource: The Declaration of Independence

"The Declaration of Independence laid the cornerstone of human government upon the first precepts of Christianity."
John Quincy Adams

There is a place to sign at the end.

In CONGRESS July 4, 1776.

The unanimous Declaration of the thirteen united States of America,

When in the course of human events, it becomes necessary for one people to dissolve the political bands which have connected them with another, and to assume among the powers of the earth, the separate and equal station to which the laws of nature and of nature's God entitle them, a decent respect to the opinions of mankind requires that they should declare the causes which impel them to the separation.

We hold these truths to be self-evident:

That all men are created equal; that they are endowed by their Creator with certain unalienable rights; that among these are life, liberty, and the pursuit of happiness; that, to secure these rights, governments are instituted among men, deriving their just powers from the consent of the governed; that whenever any form of government becomes destructive of these ends, it is the right of the people to alter or to abolish it, and to institute new government, laying its foundation on such principles, and organizing its powers in such form, as to them shall seem most likely to effect their safety and happiness. Prudence, indeed, will dictate that governments long established should not be changed for light and transient causes; and accordingly all experience hath shown that mankind are more disposed to suffer, while evils are sufferable than to right themselves by abolishing the forms to which they are accustomed. But when a long train of abuses and usurpations, pursuing invariably the same object, evinces a design to reduce them under absolute despotism, it is their right, it is their duty, to throw off such government, and to provide new guards for their future security.

Such has been the patient sufferance of these colonies; and such is now the necessity which constrains them to alter their former systems of government. The history of the present King of Great Britain is a history of repeated injuries and usurpations, all having in direct object the establishment of an absolute tyranny over these states. To prove this, let facts be submitted to a candid world.

He has refused his assent to laws, the most wholesome and necessary for the public good.

He has forbidden his governors to pass laws of immediate and pressing importance, unless suspended in their operation till his assent should be obtained; and, when so suspended, he has utterly neglected to attend to them.

He has refused to pass other laws for the accommodation of large districts of people, unless those people would relinquish the right of representation in the legislature, a right inestimable to them, and formidable to tyrants only.

He has called together legislative bodies at places unusual uncomfortable, and distant from the depository of their public records, for the sole purpose of fatiguing them into compliance with his measures.

He has dissolved representative houses repeatedly, for opposing, with manly firmness, his invasions on the rights of the people.

He has refused for a long time, after such dissolutions, to cause others to be elected; whereby the legislative powers, incapable of annihilation, have returned to the people at large for their exercise; the state remaining, in the mean time, exposed to all the dangers of invasions from without and convulsions within.

He has endeavored to prevent the population of these states; for that purpose obstructing the laws for naturalization of foreigners; refusing to pass others to encourage their migration hither, and raising the conditions of new appropriations of lands.

He has obstructed the administration of justice, by refusing his assent to laws for establishing judiciary powers.

He has made judges dependent on his will alone, for the tenure of their offices, and the amount and payment of their salaries.

He has erected a multitude of new offices, and sent hither swarms of officers to harass our people and eat out their substance.

He has kept among us, in times of peace, standing armies, without the consent of our legislatures.

He has affected to render the military independent of, and superior to, the civil power.

He has combined with others to subject us to a jurisdiction foreign to our Constitution and unacknowledged by our laws, giving his assent to their acts of pretended legislation:

For quartering large bodies of armed troops among us;

For protecting them, by a mock trial, from punishment for any murders which they should commit on the inhabitants of these states;

For cutting off our trade with all parts of the world;

For imposing taxes on us without our consent;

For depriving us, in many cases, of the benefits of trial by jury;

For transporting us beyond seas, to be tried for pretended offenses;

For abolishing the free system of English laws in a neighboring province, establishing therein an arbitrary government, and enlarging its boundaries, so as to render it at once an example and fit instrument for introducing the same absolute rule into these colonies;

For taking away our charters, abolishing our most valuable laws, and altering fundamentally the forms of our governments;

For suspending our own legislatures, and declaring themselves invested with power to legislate for us in all cases whatsoever.

He has abdicated government here, by declaring us out of his protection and waging war against us.

He has plundered our seas, ravaged our coasts, burned our towns, and destroyed the lives of our people.

He is at this time transporting large armies of foreign mercenaries to complete the works of death, desolation, and tyranny already begun with circumstances of cruelty and perfidy scarcely paralleled in the most barbarous ages, and totally unworthy the head of a civilized nation.

He has constrained our fellow-citizens, taken captive on the high seas, to bear arms against their country, to become the executioners of their friends and brethren, or to fall themselves by their hands.

He has excited domestic insurrection among us, and has endeavored to bring on the inhabitants of our frontiers the merciless Indian savages, whose known rule of warfare is an undistinguished destruction of all ages, sexes, and conditions.

In every stage of these oppressions we have petitioned for redress in the most humble terms; our repeated petitions have been answered only by repeated injury. A prince, whose character is thus marked by every act which may define a tyrant, is unfit to be the ruler of a free people.

Nor have we been wanting in our attentions to our British brethren. We have warned them, from time to time, of attempts by their legislature to extend an unwarrantable jurisdiction over us. We have reminded them of the circumstances of our emigration and settlement here. We have appealed to their native justice and magnanimity; and we have conjured them, by the ties of our common kindred, to disavow these usurpations which would inevitably interrupt our connections and correspondence. They too, have been deaf to the voice of justice and of consanguinity. We must, therefore, acquiesce in the necessity which denounces our separation, and hold them as we hold the rest of mankind, enemies in war, in peace friends.

We, therefore, the representatives of the United States of America, in General Congress assembled, appealing to the Supreme Judge of the world for the rectitude of our intentions, do, in the name and by the authority of the good people of these colonies solemnly publish and declare, That these United Colonies are, and of right ought to be, FREE AND INDEPENDENT STATES; that they are absolved from all allegiance to the British crown and that all political connection between them and the state of Great Britain is, and ought to be, totally dissolved; and that, as free and independent states, they have full power to levy war, conclude peace, contract alliances, establish commerce, and do all other acts and things which independent states may of right do. And for the support of this declaration, with a firm reliance on the protection of Divine Providence, we mutually pledge to each other our lives, our fortunes, and our sacred honor.

[Signed by] JOHN HANCOCK [President]

New Hampshire
JOSIAH BARTLETT,
WM. WHIPPLE,
MATTHEW THORNTON.

Massachusetts Bay
SAML. ADAMS,
JOHN ADAMS,
ROBT. TREAT PAINE,
ELBRIDGE GERRY.

Rhode Island
STEP. HOPKINS,
WILLIAM ELLERY.

Connecticut
ROGER SHERMAN,
SAM'EL HUNTINGTON,
WM. WILLIAMS,
OLIVER WOLCOTT.

New York
WM. FLOYD,
PHIL. LIVINGSTON,
FRANS. LEWIS,
LEWIS MORRIS.

New Jersey
RICHD. STOCKTON,
JNO. WITHERSPOON,
FRAS. HOPKINSON,
JOHN HART,
ABRA. CLARK.

Pennsylvania
ROBT. MORRIS
BENJAMIN RUSH,
BENJA. FRANKLIN,
JOHN MORTON,
GEO. CLYMER,
JAS. SMITH,
GEO. TAYLOR,
JAMES WILSON,
GEO. ROSS.

Delaware
CAESAR RODNEY,
GEO. READ,
THO. M'KEAN.

Maryland
JAMES WILSON,
SAMUEL CHASE,
WM. PACA,
THOS. STONE,
CHARLES CARROLL of
Carrollton.

Virginia
GEORGE WYTHE,
RICHARD HENRY LEE,
TH. JEFFERSON,
BENJA. HARRISON,
THS. NELSON, JR.,
FRANCIS LIGHTFOOT LEE,
CARTER BRAXTON.

North Carolina
WM. HOOPER,
JOSEPH HEWES,
JOHN PENN.

South Carolina
EDWARD RUTLEDGE,
THOS. HAYWARD, JUNR.,
THOMAS LYNCH, JUNR.,
ARTHUR MIDDLETON.

Georgia
BUTTON GWINNETT,
LYMAN HALL,
GEO. WALTON.

---

* Sign Here

REFERENCES

1 Lives Are at Stake

[1] Abraham Lincoln, Presidential Proclamation, (March 30, 1863)

[2] "Congress Has Three Days to Stop Obama's Internet Surrender", breitbart.com, September 28, 2016, www.breitbart.com/big-govern ment/2016/09/28/obamas-internet-surrender-must-be-stopped-icann

[3] "Obama Omits Creator-in Declaration of Independence," usanewsfirst.com, July 5, 2012, http://www.usanewsfirst.com/2012/07/05/obama-omits-creator-in-declaration-of-independence

[4] "Assange: Clinton is a cog for Goldman Sachs & the Saudis (JOHN PILGER EXCLUSIVE VIDEO & TRANSCRIPT)," rt.com, November 5, 2016, https://www.rt.com/news/365405-assange-pilger-full-transcript/

[5] "Churches called to pray for Christian leaders," usa.church, February 28, 2017, https://www.usa.church/churches-called-pray-christian-leaders/

[6] "THE TRUTH ABOUT THE NEW YORK BOMBING," infowars.com, September 18, 2016, http://www.infowars.com/the-truth-about-the-new-york-bombing/

[7] "Homeland Security: Fundamentalists Possible Terrorists – Anti-God Obama After Christians," *usanewsfirst.com,* July 8, 2012, http://www.usanewsfirst.com/2012/07/08/homeland-security-anti-abortion-groups-possible-terrorists-anti-god-obama-after-christians

[8] " Pamela Geller: Shocking New Details Emerge in Idaho Muslim Migrant Rape Case," breitbart.com, August 7, 2016, http://www.breitbart.com/immigration/2016/08/07/pamela-geller-shocking-new-details-emerge-idaho-muslim-migrant-rape-case/

[9] " United Airlines FORCES Woman to Switch Seats After Muslim Men DEMAND It," toprightnews.com, September 30, 2016, http://toprightnews.com/united-airlines-forces-woman-to-switch-seats-after-muslim-men-demand-it/

[10] "Kids wear red, white and blue in spite of no America Day", jhnewsandguide.com, October 1, 2015, http://www.jhnewsandguide.com /news/schools/kids-wear-red-white-and-blue-in-spite-of-no/article_887a4633-8d20-55ba-afbf-8130d199867c.html

[11] "Donald J. Trump Statement on Preventing Muslim Immigration," usa.church, December 7, 2015, https://www.donaldjtrump.com/press-releases/donald-j.-trump-statement-on-preventing-muslim-immigration

[12] "Fewer US-Born Americans Have Jobs Now Than In 2007," dailycaller.com, December, 19, 2014, http://dailycaller.com/2014/12/19/fewer-us-born-americans-have-jobs-now-than-in-2007/

[13] wnd.com, December 22, 2009, http://www.wnd.com/2009/12/119800/

[14] "Empire State Building honors China in lights," nbcnews.com, September 30, 2009, http://www.nbcnews.com/id/33100000/ns/us_news-life/t/empire-state-building-honors-china-lights/

[15] "U.S. and Chinese troops connect in first-ever exchange at JBLM," thenewstribune.com, Nov. 20, 2015, http://bit.ly/1Sc8jSV

[16] "Justice Department Spies on Millions of Cars: WSJ," *msn.com,* January 27, 2015, http://bit.ly/1IAYBF1

[17] "NSA Spies on Americans Through Your TV with FLAME Spy Program," *usanewsfirst.com,* August 6, 2013, http://www.usanewsfirst.com/2013/08/06/nsa-spies-on-americans-through-your-tv-with-flame-spy-program/

[18] "Traditional-marriage 'hero' Roy Moore removed from office," wnd.com, September 30, 2016, http://www.wnd.com/2016/09/traditional-marriage-hero-roy-moore-removed-from-office

[19] "Mike Huckabee: We Must Stand with Kim Davis Against 'Criminalization of Christianity', breitbart.com, September 7, 2015, http://bit.ly/1Lfftkm

[20] "Same-Sex Marriage Ruling Is Another Roe v. Wade," beitbart.com, June 26, 2015, http://dailysignal.com/2015/07/02/state-silences-bakers-who-refused-to-make-cake-for-lesbian-couple-fines-them-135k

[21] "Same-sex Marriage Is Not Law, Says Mike Huckabee," usa.church, November 14, 2015, https://www.usa.church/2015/11/14/same-sex-marriage-is-not-law-says-mike-huckabee/

[22] "Corporations threaten boycott over Georgia, North Carolina legislation seen as "anti gay"," fox6now.com, March 27, 2016, http://fox6now.com/2016/03/27/corporations-threaten-boycott-over-georgia-north-carolina-legislation-seen-as-anti-gay/

[23] "Men Flood Target to Film Teen Girls after Allowing Males in Female Changing Rooms," freedomoutpost.com, June 18, 2016, http://freedomoutpost.com/men-flood-target-to-film-teen-girls-after-allowing-males-in-female-changing-rooms/

[24] Noah Webster, History of the United States, (New-Haven..., 1832), 326-327

[25] "U.S. Achievement Stalls as Other Nations Make Gains," edweek.com, Dec. 3, 2013, http://www.edweek.org/ew/articles/2013/12/03/14pisa.h33.html

[26] " Trump: Unshackle Churches From Johnson Amendment," dailywire.com, October 3, 2016, http://www.dailywire.com/news/9649/trump-unshackle-churches-johnson-amendment-robert-kraychik#

[27] "For Many American States, It's Like the Recession Never Ended," bloomberg.com, accessed May 20, 2015, http://www.bloomberg.com/news/articles/2015-05-20/six-years-into-recovery-u-s-states-struggle-to-balance-budgets

[28] "40 percent of unemployed have quit looking for jobs," cnbc.com, accessed May 20, 2015, http://www.cnbc.com/id/102694868

[29] Charles Francis Adams, The Works of John Adams, Second President..., Volume 9, (Boston, Charles C. Little and James Brown, 1854), 169

[30] John Winthrop, A Model of Christian Charity, (1630)

[31] The New York Sabbath Committee, First Five Years of the Sabbath Reform, 1857-62, (New York, Edward O. Jenkins, Printer, 1862), 43

2 First Truth—Covenant with the One True God

[1] Dr. Paul Jehle, Plymouth Rock Foundation, "July 2012 E News," *plymrock.org,* July, 2012, http://www.plymrock.org/july2012news.php

[2] The Pilgrims, Mayflower Compact, (November 11, 1620)

[3] John Winthrop, A Model of Christian Charity, (1630)

[4] Yale Law School, "The Articles of Confederation of the United Colonies of New England; May 19, 1643," *avalon.law.yale.edu,* accessed January 12, 2015, http://avalon.law.yale.edu/17th_century/art1613.asp

[5] Alexander Biddle, Old Family Letters: Copied from the Originals, (Philadelphia, J. P. Lippincott Company, 1892), 248-249

[6] Library of Congress, "Religion and the Founding of the American Republic," acc. January 12, 2015, *loc.gov,* http://www.loc.gov/exhibits/religion/rel04.html

[7] "11% of All Christians in the world Live in the USA," *usanewsfirst.com,* June 19, 2015, http://www.usanewsfirst.com/2015/06/13/11-of-all-christians-live-in-the-usa

[7] John C. Fitzpatrick, The Writings of George Washington from the Original Manuscript Sources 1745-1799 Volume 15 May 6, 1779-July 28, 1779, (Library of Congress, 1939), 55

[8] "Christians Greatly Outnumber All Others in the USA," *usanewsfirst.com,* June 13, 2015, http://bit.ly/1ebf5KS

[9] John Whiting and Henry Whiting, Revolutionary Orders of General Washington: Issued During the Years 1778, '80, '81, & '82 (New York and London, Wiley and Putnam, 1844) 32

[10] Benjamin Franklin Morris, Christian Life and Character of the Civil Institutions of the United States..., (Cincinnati, George W. Childs, 1864), 557

[11] Gallup CEO Jim Clifton Interview on Fox News, *youtube.com,* February 5, 2015, https://www.youtube.com/watch?v=CTRAibMiLZ8

[12] "It's official: America is now No. 2," *marketwatch.com,* December 4, 2014, http://www.marketwatch.com/story/its-official-america-is-now-no-2-2014-12-04, and

"Does size matter? China poised to overtake US as world's largest economy in 2014," *ft.com,* April 30, 2014, http://blogs.ft.com/the-world/2014/04/does-size-matter-china-poised-to-overtake-us-as-worlds-largest-economy-in-2014/

[13] "144 Years of Marriage and Divorce Rates in U.S. (from CDC)," rhiever.github.io, November 11, 2016, http://rhiever.github.io/marriage-divorce-stats/marriages_divorces_per_capita.html

[14] "Unmarried Childbearing," www.cdc.gov, Accessed 11/13/16, http://www.cdc.gov/nchs/fastats/unmarried-childbearing.htm, and "Nonmarital Childbearing in the United States, 1940–99," www.cdc.gov, Acc. 11/13/16, https://www.cdc.gov/nchs/data/nvsr/nvsr48/nvs48_16.pdf

[15] Noah Webster, Letters to a Young Gentleman Commencing His Education..., (New Haven, Howe and Spalding, 1823), 7

[16] John Hancock, Massachusetts Governor's Proclamation, (October 15, 1791)

[17] George Washington, Presidential Proclamation, (October 3, 1789)

3 American Secrets for Safe and Blessed Lives

[1] John Witherspoon, The Works of the Reverend John Witherspoon Vol. III, (Philadelphia, William W. Woodward, 1802), 42

[2] Benjamin Franklin Morris, Christian Life and Character of the Civil Institutions of the United..., (Cincinnati, George W. Childs, 1864), 337

[3] Yale Law School, "The Articles of Confederation of the United Colonies of New England; May 19, 1643," *avalon.law.yale.edu,* accessed January 12, 2015, http://avalon.law.yale.edu/17th_century/art1613.asp

[4] Abraham Lincoln, Presidential Proclamation, (March 30, 1863)

[5] Amos Blanchard, American Military and Naval Biography: Containing... the Officers of the Revolution, (Cincinnati, A. Salisbury, 1832), 476

[6] Sir William Blackstone, Commentaries on the Laws of England: In Four Books... Volume 1, (New York, W. E. Dean, 1838), 94

[7] Sir William Blackstone, Commentaries on the Laws of England: In the Order, and Compiled from... (London, Saunders and Benning, 1840), 20

[8] The Law Journal for 1806; Consisting of Original Communications..., (London, W. Clarke and Sons, 1807), 106

[9] Samuel Adams, The Writings of Samuel Adams: 1770-1773, (New York, G. P. Putnam's Sons, 1906), 355

[10] Benjamin Franklin Morris, Christian Life and Character of the Civil Institutions of the United..., (Cincinnati, George W. Childs, 1864), 337

[11] Joseph Story, Commentaries on the Constitution of the United States: With a ..., Volume 3, (Boston, Hilliard, Gray, and Company, 1833), 728

[12] John Torrey Morse, American Statesmen: John Marshall Vol. X, (Boston and New York, Houghton, Mifflin and Company, 1899), 253

[13] John Profatt, The American Decisions: Cases of General Value and Authority Volume 1, (San Francisco, Bancroft-Whitney Co., 1910), 417

[14] Noah Webster, History of the United States, (New-Haven..., 1832), 299-300

[27] Library of Congress, "Religion and the Founding of the American Republic," acc. March 2, 2015, *loc.gov,* http://www.loc.gov/exhibits/religion/rel06-2.html

4 Second Truth—Seek and Find God

[1] Benjamin Franklin Morris, Christian Life and Character of the Civil Institutions of the United States..., (Cincinnati, George W. Childs, 1864), 328, and Reports of Committees of the House of Representatives Made During the First Session..., (Washington: A. O. P. Nicholson, 1854)

[2] Robert Baird, Religion of the United States of America, (Glasgow and Edinburgh, Blackie and Son, 1844), 263, and Journals of the American Congress...1774-1788, Vol. I, (Washington: Way and Gideon, 1823), 309-310

5 Third Truth—Living the Bible Way

[1] Sir William Blackstone, Commentaries on the Laws of England: In Four Books..., (Philadelphia, J.B. Lippincott & Co., 1859), Page 28

[2] W. C. Anderson, Review of Dr. Scott's Bible and Politics in the Light of Religion and the Law, (San Francisco, Towne and Bacon, 1858), 75

[3] Williams Jay, The Life of John Jay: With Selections from His Correspondence and ..., Volume 2, (New York, J. & J. Harper, 1833), 351

[4] Abraham Lincoln, Complete Works Comprising his Speeches, Letters, State Papers, and Miscellaneous Writings Vol. Two, John Nicolay and John Hay, (New York: The Century Co., 1894), 574

6 Fourth Truth—Jesus Rules the Nation

[1] Elizabeth Cooper, Popular History of America..., (London: Longman, Green, Longman, Roberts, & Green, 1865), 399

[2] George Washington, Presidential Proclamation, (October 3, 1789)

[3] Junius Brutus, A Defense of Liberty Against Tyrants, *nlnrac.org*, (1579, English Richard Baldwin 1689, accessed January 23, 2015),http://www.nlnrac.org/classical/late-medieval-transformations/documents/defense

[4] Jonathan Mayhew, A Discourse Concerning Unlimited Submission and Non-resistance to the Higher Powers, (1750), 25

7 Fifth Truth—Hearts to Be Like Jesus

[1] Abraham Lincoln, Presidential Proclamation, (March 30, 1863)

[2] Supreme Court, Church of the Holy Trinity v. United States, (Feb. 29, 1892)

[3] "Noah Webster," webstersdictionary1828.com, Accessed January 24, 2015, http://webstersdictionary1828.com/NoahWebster

[4] John C. Fitzpatrick, The Writings of George Washington from the Original Manuscript Sources 1745-1799, Vol. 15, (Library of Congress, 1939), 55

[5] W. C. Anderson, Review of Dr. Scott's Bible and Politics in the Light of Religion and the Law, (San Francisco, Towne and Bacon, 1858), 75

[6] American Missionary Society, The American Missionary, Vol. 20, (January 1876), 183

[7] William Vincent Wells, The Life and Public Services of Samuel Adams..., Vol. 2, (Boston, Little, Brown and Co., 1865), 223

8 Sixth Truth—Victory Over Sin

[1] "Mormon founder Joseph Smith had as many as 40 wives," *news.yahoo.com,* November 11, 2014, http://news.yahoo.com/mormon-founder-joseph-smith-had-many-40-wives-212016652.html

[2] "Where Are the Christian Leaders? Pastors & the Mormon Cult," usanewsfirst.com, acc. Dec. 19, 2015, http://www.usanewsfirst.com/2014/12/16/where-are-the-christian-leaders-pastors-the-mormon-cult

[3] "Who's On the LORD's Side," usa.church, acc. December 19, 2015, https://www.usa.church/whos-on-the-lords-side/

[4] John Whiting and Henry Whiting, Revolutionary Orders of General Washington: Issued During the Years 1778, '80, '81, & '82 (New York and London, Wiley and Putnam, 1844) 32

[5] "Prevalence and Awareness of HIV Infection Among Men Who Have Sex With Men..." cdc.gov, September 24, 2010, http://www.cdc.gov/mmwr/preview/mmwrhtml/mm5937a2.htm

[6] "New Study Shows Homosexuals Live 20 Fewer Years," *freerepublic.com,* June 6, 2005, http://www.freerepublic.com/focus/news/1417935/posts

[7] "Mike Huckabee blasts same-sex marriage ruling," foxnews.com, June 29, 2015, http://www.foxnews.com/transcript/2015/06/29/mike-huckabee-blasts-same-sex-marriage-ruling

[8] "GAO Confirms... Abortion Advocates Spent About $1.5 Billion in Tax Dollars," *cnsnews.com,* March 26, 2015, http://bit.ly/1ODgTdg

10 Covenant Protection, Blessings, and Favor

[1] Yale Law School, "The Articles of Confederation of the United Colonies of New England; May 19, 1643," *avalon.law.yale.edu,* accessed January 12, 2015, http://avalon.law.yale.edu/17th_century/art1613.asp

Prayer of Salvation

To become a Christian, pray a prayer like this:

Father,

I thank You that Jesus Christ died on the cross to forgive my sins. I confess with my mouth the Lord Jesus and I believe in my heart that You raised Jesus from the dead. I ask You for the Holy Spirit. In Jesus' name. Amen. (John 3:16, Romans 10:9-10)

To grow as a Christian, pray and read the Holy Bible daily. I recommend reading a chapter or more in the morning and a chapter or more before sleeping. Then think about Bible verses during the day.

Across the nation, people ask me what Bible version I use. I love the King James Version (KJV).

If you prayed to be a Christian, let me know at USA Christian Church. The website is:

www.USA.church

Books by Steven Andrew

JESUS MAKES AMERICA GREAT™

Paperback: ISBN 9780998668291
eBook: ISBN 9780998668284

"Jesus Makes America Great" is a condensed and fast reading version of "Save America" that focuses on making the USA great again.

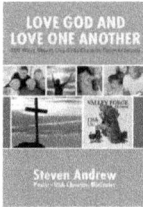

Love God and Love One Another

Paperback: ISBN 9780977955039
eBook: ISBN 9780977955084

Making A Strong Christian Nation

Paperback: ISBN 9780977955077

Check for these upcoming new books:

The American Disciple Making Team™ **Handbook**

Are You an American?

One Million Americans on the LORD's Side

If you believe JESUS MAKES AMERICA GREAT, I invite you to join *One Million Americans on the LORD's Side* at www.USA.church.

One Million Americans
On the LORD's Side
Saving the USA

"Blessed is the nation whose God is the LORD" Psalm 33:12

Become a Partner, T-shirts, Coffee Mugs, and Items to Help Share the Gospel

To become a monthly partner or to give a one-time gift to USA Christian Church to help make the USA exceptional, and for a full list of apparel and other products, see www.USA.church. The proceeds go to sharing the Gospel.

JESUS
MAKES

AMERICA
GREAT™

www.ingramcontent.com/pod-product-compliance
Lightning Source LLC
LaVergne TN
LVHW051100080426
835508LV00019B/1984